Retooling
HR

Also by John Boudreau

Beyond HR: The New Science of Human Capital,
with Peter M. Ramstad

Retooling
HR

Using Proven Business Tools
to Make Better Decisions
About Talent

John W. Boudreau

HARVARD BUSINESS PRESS

Boston, Massachusetts

Copyright 2010 Harvard Business School Publishing Corporation
All rights reserved
Printed in the United States of America

14 13 12 11 10   5 4 3 2 1

No part of this publication may be reproduced, stored in or introduced into
a retrieval system, or transmitted, in any form, or by any means (electronic,
mechanical, photocopying, recording, or otherwise), without the prior
permission of the publisher. Requests for permission should be directed to
permissions@hbsp.harvard.edu, or mailed to Permissions, Harvard Business
School Publishing, 60 Harvard Way, Boston, Massachusetts 02163.

Library of Congress Cataloging-in-Publication Data

Boudreau, John W.
  Retooling HR : using proven business tools to make better decisions about
talent / John W. Boudreau.
    p. cm.
  ISBN 978-1-4221-3007-0 (hardcover : alk. paper)   1. Personnel
management.   2. Human capital.   3. Organizational effectiveness.   I. Title.
  HF5549.B7726 2010
  658.3'01—dc22

                                                                      2010000931

The paper used in this publication meets the requirements of the American
National Standard for Permanence of Paper for Publications and Documents
in Libraries and Archives Z39.48-1992.

*To my father, whose admirable dedication
to work and family first kindled my fascination with the
human side of the workplace, and who always had just the
right tool for the job.*

*To my mother, whose empathy and irreverence reveal playful
discovery in even the toughest work.*

Contents

Acknowledgments   *ix*

Introduction: Better Talent Models Lead to Better
Talent Decisions   1

   The Hidden Power for HR in Using Proven Business Models

1 Using Performance Optimization to Retool
   Work Analysis   25

      From Job Descriptions, Competencies, and KPIs to
      Return on Improved Performance

2 Using Portfolio Diversification to Retool Talent Scenarios   57

      From the Right Talent for the Future to Talent Hedging
      Against a Risky Future

3 Using Consumer Research to Retool Talent
   Supply Strategies   89

      From Let's Make an iDeal to Optimized Talent Segmentation

4 Using Inventory Optimization to Retool Talent
   Gap Analysis   121

      From Turnover and Hiring to Talent Inventory

5   Using Workforce Logistics to Retool the
    Talent Life Cycle   149

    From Mapping How People Move to Optimizing
    Talent Networks

6   Retooled HR: From Risk-Minimizing Administrator
    to Risk-Optimizing Partner   179

    Making Organizations More Adept and Accountable
    for Talent

Notes   195

Index   201

About the Author   213

Acknowledgments

This book, as all my work, benefits from the valuable insights of my colleagues in the organizations I have been privileged to work with, my academic community, and the many students who have taught me so much over the years. These individuals made particularly generous contributions to this book: At the Center for Effective Organizations, my colleagues Ed Lawler, Alec Levenson, Theresa Welbourne, and especially Jessica Schoner. At Towers Perrin: Linda David, Ravin Jesuthasan, Max Caldwell, and Roselyn Feinsod. My colleagues who are HR leaders, including: John Bronson; Mayank Jain at Ameriprise; Paige Ross and Lucien Alziari at Avon; Jean Jackson at Baystate Health; Alan May at Boeing; Terry Gray at Cargill; Jay Moldenhauer-Salazar and Eva Sage-Gavin at Gap, Inc.; Prasad Setty at Google; Bina Chaurasia at HP; David White, Andrea de Young, Scott Pitasky, Alexis Fink, and Rupert Bader at Microsoft; Ian Ziskin and Michele Toth at Northrop Grumman; Mike Stafford at Starbucks; Beat Meyer at UBS; and Peter Attfield and Sandy Ogg at Unilever. My academic colleagues: Wayne Cascio, Denise Rousseau, and Ken Schultz. A special thanks to the team at Harvard Business Publishing, including Brian Surrette, Ania Wieckowski, Allison Peter, and Melinda Merino.

Introduction

Better Talent Models Lead to Better Talent Decisions

The Hidden Power for HR in

Using Proven Business Models

In October 2008, I spoke at an event that included an on-stage interview with Jack Welch, former CEO of GE. Welch spoke about the growing evidence of an impending downturn, and when asked for his most important advice to leaders, he said that the coming economic challenges meant hard choices for companies, often involving workforce cuts. It meant that in many organizations, the top performers would miss the performance targets that would normally trigger bonuses, incentives, and stock options. Welch admonished leaders to put aside a "bucket of money" to fund signals to the most vital employees about how much they were valued, because "your competitors will be at your doorstep waiting for them to become disillusioned and leave you." This remarkable quotation vividly demonstrates the priority business leaders place on talent.

But later, as I was working with a group of top HR leaders at the event, I reminded them of Welch's remarks. I asked them, "How many of your organizations have HR and line leaders who can reliably and logically identify which of your employees are vital, and how big that bucket of money will need to be, and what you need to do with it, to retain the vital talent you need?" Only a few hands went up.

The HR leaders at the meeting were members of fine organizations that had world-class HR systems in place to retain and reward their vital talent. However, even with those systems, they could not be certain that their leaders could logically and reliably direct limited talent resources where they would be most vital and most effective.

In contrast, the same HR leaders knew that their organizational leaders used consistent logical frameworks to analyze where to invest, maintain, or cut resources such as technology, manufacturing, and marketing, using principles such as net present value, production optimization, and market segmentation. These frameworks do not produce perfect decisions, nor are they blessed with perfect measures and information. Yet they provide immense value. First, they enable functional experts in marketing, technology, and finance to better understand and articulate the effects of their decisions and programs on organization success. Second, and perhaps much more important, such frameworks allow stakeholders, such as unit managers and organization leaders to better forecast, and be held accountable for, the full effect of their own decisions about these important resources.

Consider the value of the supply chain as a framework that yields transparency and accountability. A simple diagram can show how products on the shelf must first proceed through a pathway that includes design, raw materials sourcing, manufacturing, assembly, distribution, sales, and service. If salespeople choose to frantically book sales at the end of the month to make their quota, the supply-chain system can show how the spike in sales ripples through all the other processes, often producing large cost increases, quality problems, or delays. The salespeople who frantically book sales are not trying to cause problems; they are merely responding to the part of the supply chain they see and are held accountable for. Similar examples exist up and down the supply chain, where maximizing one part can damage the larger system. Manufacturing managers want facilities running at full utilization to minimize their cost per item, but setting production levels high enough for full utilization can produce more than the distribution and sales systems can handle. Distribution managers want every delivery on time and complete, but to gain these qualities they may hold more inventory than the pricing can justify.

Without the supply-chain framework, such consequences are difficult to see and articulate. With that framework, the consequences are clearer, accountability is more complete, and better decisions get made. The power of the supply-chain framework is that in one simple idea, it allows everyone affected to understand the full picture. Salespeople, manufacturing managers, and distribution leaders can be held accountable not only for their own part of the supply chain but also for the full effect of their decisions. This widely accepted tool, then, aids in communication and in the optimization of the entire sales and distribution system.

A more subtle effect of the supply-chain framework is how it magnifies the impact and value of the supply-chain function and its experts. The supply-chain function designs the logic and the metaphors and signals that go to unit leaders. When unit leaders use its systems, the logic, signals, and metaphors make the bigger picture, and their accountability in it, more visible. Supply-chain functional experts build the system, but it is the unit managers, salespeople, and others that use the system to make better decisions.

Retooling HR means taking these kinds of proven business tools, which are already used by decision makers, and adapting them to HR to optimize an organization's entire talent management system. Retooling HR improves vital decisions about people in three ways.

First, the logic and rigor of proven business frameworks from disciplines such as finance, marketing, and operations management offer untapped opportunities to improve how HR organizations analyze, report, and optimize human resources. Second, when HR leaders recast decisions about people using proven business tools, these decisions become more engaging and understandable for non-HR leaders, because they are accustomed to using these business tools for other resources. Third, when decisions about human capital are recast in the language and logic of proven business frameworks, leaders outside of HR can use these new frameworks to be held accountable, more transparently and effectively, for the impact of their human capital decisions.

How Improved Models Improve Talent Decisions

At first glance, it's easy to think that smart leaders are already making good decisions about human capital. Most organization leaders have long ago realized that their people—or talent or human capital—are important and vital. Most leaders are eager to make great decisions about their people and to have their colleagues in the HR profession help them. HR's stakeholders are often willing to invest millions in HR information systems, leadership development programs, and global competency or performance management systems. They pore over HR data on turnover, cycle time, engagement, and performance, searching for connections to their business outcomes that will help them improve their talent and performance. They individually commit to weeding out the bottom 10 percent, or increasing employee engagement scores, or identifying four successors to each position.

At first glance, it also appears that the HR function in most organizations is effectively supporting decisions about human capital. HR leaders are trusted advisers to business leaders. HR programs reflect best-in-class examples and often are supported with data that shows their effects on learning, performance, and even financial outcomes. HR systems produce scorecards, drill-down reports, and heat maps showing virtually every employee characteristic arrayed against almost any business or performance indicator. In the HR profession, the use of data and benchmarking, and the degree of systems sophistication, has never been higher.

Yet below the surface, decisions about talent and human capital are often made by leaders without well-understood frameworks that show how their decisions connect to affected systems outside their immediate unit. Suppose that your organization's projected long-term growth will require a 50 percent increase in product design capabilities and that it takes about three years from the time they are hired, to develop good product design engineers. A unit manager in the design engineering department is given several goals, including completing this year's design projects, keeping costs in line, and hiring six new engineers.

Suppose that the unit manager completes all the projects and hires only three engineers. How would your performance and budgeting systems react? Often, the unit manager is congratulated, because he completed all the projects and spent only half the projected budget for design engineers. From an accounting standpoint, this is logical. But a more complete perspective reveals that by failing to hire the additional three engineers, the unit manager has put the organization behind in its pipeline for needed future design engineers and made it more likely that the organization will be unprepared in five years.

The unit manager is aware of the long-term goal of preparing enough engineers to meet future growth, but he has little visibility or accountability for it. HR leaders are often keenly aware of the long-term effects, but even when those effects are reflected in HR plans and budgets, they are not present in the language of the business units. Yet if this same manager had chosen to invest only half the budgeted projected amount for the first year of a five-year manufacturing construction project, the supply chain would identify the long-term effects. The framework would also hold the unit manager accountable, and the unit manager would better understand the implications of his decision, and likely he would improve it.

This kind of thing happens all the time. HR requires unit managers to remove or improve the bottom 10 percent of their employees, but when unit leaders find that their bottom 10 percent are productive workers who are hard to replace, they resist. They see the substantial disruption caused by the 10 percent rule in their unit, and they try to minimize that disruption. Is the larger benefit of the rule really worth the disruption to the unit? Such questions are often challenging for HR and its stakeholders. Yet, engineers routinely tackle such questions by analyzing the relationship between performance and results. The well-understood metaphor is to require very tight quality tolerances where they matter a lot, and allow them to be looser where they matter less.

In another example, HR works with business forecasters to predict gaps and hiring needs. The department builds recruitment plans that balance quality, timing, and cost, based on projected business activity and talent demand. Yet when business unit leaders encounter unexpected spikes in activity, they ask their HR business partners to fill the vacancies as soon as possible. The HR business partners meet the goal, and are heralded as being responsive business partners, but they may do it by tapping recruitment sources that are more expensive or of lower quality. If this were an inventory of finished goods, unit leaders would work with inventory planners to calculate the costs of shortages in light of the larger disruption to the inventory and sourcing plan. If the disruption or cost to the sourcing process are high, unit leaders accept and are held accountable for how their reaction to shortages affects the larger system, and they realize the right decision may be to live with the shortage, not insist on reducing it. Experts in the inventory function along with the unit managers combine to make better decisions.

Retooling Enhances the Strengths of HR

The ideas in this book are meant to build on, and not substitute for, the systems, frameworks, and professional contributions that HR provides. Recall the group of HR leaders at the conference, who were not all certain that their business leaders would know how to answer Jack Welch's question. The remarkable thing was that these HR leaders were among the best in their field and had built and led HR functions that were justifiably respected, influential, and award-winning. Yet there was a striking contrast between the way their leaders would approach tough personnel decisions and the approach they would take toward other resources.

Talent Investments in the Global Economic Downturn?

The 2008–2009 economic downturn suggests that when the chips were down, business leaders were quick to cut talent investments. The annual Conference Board CEO Challenge Survey asks hundreds of senior executives from around the world to identify and rate their most pressing concerns. The report described the relegation of talent management: "The headline of *The Conference Board CEO Challenge 2007: Top 10 Challenges* report (R-1406-07-RR) was the importance of the human factor . . . Going into the autumn crisis . . . CEOs' focus on HR-related challenges was already weakening. Top management succession, for example, was already on its way down, dropping eight rankings between 2007 and July/August of 2008. The crisis may mean that now a number of these people-concerns fade from view altogether."[a] The only people elements that rose were "cost of employee health care benefits" (which jumped eleven places) and "employee efficiency" (which rose three places). Examples of those that fell the farthest (and how far they fell) were "top management succession" (eleven ranks); "corporate reputation for desirable employer or employer of choice"

The HR leaders and their stakeholders fully recognized the vital importance of decisions such as where to cut talent and where to grow it, how to optimize investments in a reduced array of incentives, and where to preserve talent investments to be prepared for the upturn. They would eventually make those decisions, but would their HR frameworks be as consistent, logical, and effective as their frameworks for money, customers, and technology? Would (ten ranks); "finding a qualified skilled workforce" (eight ranks); and "finding qualified managerial talent" (eight ranks).[b] Did the economic downturn reveal that top business leaders believe that when times get tough they can pay less attention to finding, keeping, and developing a top workforce, and more attention to making people efficient and reducing their benefits?

Yet, one year later, in August 2009, the business press was full of admonishments regarding the buyers' market in talent and the importance of hanging on to top talent as other employers begin to see signs of recovery and might poach the best talent. In two years, talent shot up to top priority, dropped down to low priority and then shot up again. This kind of volatility can be harmful, considering that people are vital and that it takes a long time to acquire and develop them. Although leaders have cut in areas such as technology, marketing, and manufacturing, these priorities don't seem to vary as much over time. Perhaps it's because business leaders have frameworks in these areas that better help them see the long-term view.

a. Linda Barrington, Ellen Hexter, and Charles Mitchell, *CEO Challenge 2008: Top 10 Challenges—Financial Crisis Edition*, Research Report R-1440-08-RR (New York: Conference Board, November 2008), 6.

b. Ibid., exhibit 3, 9.

their stakeholders respond as readily to discussions of employee turnover, pay and benefits, and career paths as they would respond to discussions about inventory, consumer preferences, and supply chains? If not, then why not?

Is it because human capital decisions matter less to organization leaders? No. Indeed, every leader in the world knows that human capital decisions like these, multiplied over tens or thousands of managers, can have effects at least as significant as decisions about manufacturing, supply chains and logistics.

Is it because human behavior is just so random or self-interested that any attempt to be systematic about it is doomed to failure? No. Human nature is just as much at work in manufacturing and marketing as it is in job performance, turnover, and careers. Indeed, a hundred years of research on work behavior actually has a lot to say about predicting things like performance and turnover.

Is it because people are not widgets, and out of respect for their free will and humanity it's unfair or wrong to use the same logic for workforce decisions as we use for decisions about more inanimate objects like inventories and machines? No. In fact, it's arguably more unfair and disrespectful to employees and job applicants to make important decisions about where to invest in their development, performance, and careers in less rigorous ways than those applied to more traditional resources.

No one intentionally tries to force worker performance improvements where they are less impactful, or to make their production numbers by overspending and underselecting employees to fill vacancies quickly. That kind of misallocation of investments happens when smart and well-meaning people respond to the best signals they have, but those signals are faulty. When the line of sight to the larger issues is fuzzy, it's easy to believe you are getting a lot done when you are actually not moving the needle—or even causing harm. Could leaders in HR, and their stakeholders, develop frameworks to make human capital decision makers more accountable and adept?

Yes, and the path is right in front of us, hidden within the logical frameworks that leaders already use for resources like money, advertising, manufacturing systems, information systems, and product components. HR is based on some of the most rigorous and analytically sophisticated methods in the social sciences, but often these tools and analysis frameworks are the sole purview of HR professionals or even of a few PhD analysts in the HR function. For decades, the question, "How can we get business leaders to use our research?" has been a perennial concern at professional meetings of industrial psychologists, researchers in HR, and HR professional societies. The answer may be that it is crucial not only to enhance the sophistication of HR frameworks but also to make them accessible to those outside HR. HR professionals need to consider how to connect HR questions to the frameworks that business leaders already know, use, and trust. In addition, by making these connections, HR leaders and analysts can open up an array of proven analytical tools that can enhance their own rigor, insights, and ability to optimize talent decisions. This book is about uncovering that hidden potential for HR and its stakeholders.

The Need to Retool HR

This book has two goals: first, I want to invite HR professionals to enhance their own analysis, communication, and decision making by making greater use of proven business tools. Second, I want to enhance the communication between HR leaders and their stakeholders by reframing HR issues through the lens of proven business frameworks that stakeholders already use and understand.

We use the expression *talent pipeline* to indicate how talent flows into, through, and out of the organization along multiple pathways, much as crude oil flows from far-flung oil fields to pipelines and refineries, or raw materials or in-process inventory flow through multiple routes. We refer to workforce separations as *turnover* because employees leave and must be replaced, much as inventory turns over as it is depleted and replaced over time. We refer to the leadership *portfolio* because the capabilities of leaders can be combined to fit future scenarios, much as a financial portfolio is built of asset classes that combine to optimize risk and returns in an uncertain future. Yet the power of business models such as logistics, inventory optimization, and portfolio theory is seldom fully exploited when we address decisions about human resources.

It's a paradox. HR leaders spend time learning finance, marketing, and other business disciplines in an effort to understand the connections between decisions about human capital and their effects on resources such as money, technology, manufacturing, and marketing. Yet decisions about acquiring, developing, deploying, and engaging talent often reflect only an HR perspective. Turnover is presented with HR definitions and calculations. Workforce flows are presented in terms of job titles, succession charts, and headcount reports. Leadership capabilities are presented in terms of competency levels and development experiences. These are valuable and insightful tools, and they are often rich in data and mathematics. However, they often bear little resemblance to the logical models that leaders use when they make decisions about inventory turnover, logistics flows, and financial portfolios. More important, they often fail to show important larger connections, and the result is that well-meaning and smart leaders make suboptimal human capital decisions.

This book shows how HR can improve its own rigor and meet its stakeholders where they are, by better tapping in to the models those leaders use for other resources. A 2009 *BusinessWeek* item made precisely this point: "Companies can now model and optimize operations, and can calculate the return on investment on everything from corporate jets to Super Bowl ads. These successes have led to the next math project: the worker. 'You have to bring the same rigor you bring to operations and finance to the analysis of people,' says Rupert Bader, director of workforce planning at Microsoft."[1] The rigor of operations and finance exists not only in the *data* that finance and operations have developed but more fundamentally in their *logical tools*, such as net present value and constraint analysis.

Most studies of HR metrics show that employee turnover is the most frequently reported human capital measure. Yet the models that leaders outside HR use to understand turnover rates are often rudimentary at best and misleading at worst.

For example, in 2005 Walmart had a turnover rate of 44 percent, close to the retail average, but turnover rates range by industry from around 15 percent to 50 percent or higher. With 1.8 million employees, each year Walmart must recruit, hire, and train more than 790,000 employees just to stay even.[2] Most leaders, confronted with a turnover rate, can clearly see the costs of replacing the departing employees and can calculate million-dollar savings from reducing turnover even a little. This is logical, and not wrong; Walmart could undoubtedly save millions of dollars per year by reducing turnover. But a look at the bigger picture leads to a far different conclusion, as discussed in chapter 4.

Indeed, when I ask business leaders what employee turnover means, they almost always initially respond that turnover is costly and should be reduced to benchmark levels. However, most HR leaders know that this is not the whole story. They would want to consider an array of additional questions, such as, How much would it cost to reduce turnover? What if those leaving were less qualified or motivated than those that might replace them? What if the cost of replacing the departing employees were a lot less than the cost of keeping them? Is it possible to recharge the organization with properly managed turnover?

The turnover rate, then, masks numerous relevant considerations. Indeed, HR systems can often provide detailed turnover reports that break down whether exiting employees are top performers, how long it takes to fill a vacancy, what departure factors they report in exit interviews, and so on.

Yet even smart business leaders often ignore this data in their efforts to reduce turnover and cut its cost. Why don't they insist on a richer discussion that could uncover the more nuanced possibilities?

Mental Models Matter

A *mental model* is the logical way someone approaches a problem or considers how things connect. For example, most leaders have a mental model of investment value that incorporates the elements of net present value, including future inflows of value, outflows of costs, their timing, a risk factor, and the principle that future benefits and costs should be discounted to reflect the fact that things received sooner are more valuable. When leaders are confronted with personnel decisions, what are their mental models?

Jeffrey Pfeffer addresses statements by the CEO of American Airlines in the mid-1990s, who wanted "to see the corpse" of whoever caused a plane to be late, creating a culture of "fear and infighting as people and units tried to pin the blame for problems on others."[3] Research shows that practicing managers' decisions reflect their assumptions about human nature, which shape their philosophies of corporate management. Those assumptions are largely driven by economics, Pfeffer tells us in another article: "The managers assumed that people are self interested, may engage in self-interest seeking with guile, and are effort averse so that they require incentives and monitoring to ensure performance."[4]

It's not that such assumptions are always wrong, but they are less precise and complete than they could be. I teach a class for MBAs titled "Motivation and Performance," which is organized around six proven theories about human motivation, including the power of groups and shared vision, norms of equity and fairness, and clear goals.[5] The idea is to help MBAs develop a comprehensive mental model of motivation at work so that they can recognize when assumptions like "people are averse to working hard and must be watched to be sure they perform" might not apply.

HR Is a Stronger Strategic Partner When HR Stakeholders Are Sophisticated

Connecting HR decisions to familiar and trusted business frameworks is a way to help leaders recognize the value of understanding HR principles such as motivation, learning, engagement, and organization design. For example, if leaders understand that the payoff of segmenting employees based on their preferences for different rewards is just like the payoff of segmenting customers based on their preferences for differential product features, then non-HR leaders may be receptive to understanding the principles of employee needs and motivation. As it turns out, evidence suggests that when business leaders are sophisticated in such HR arenas, HR is a stronger strategic partner.

Table I-1 shows the results of a survey of non-HR leaders. They were asked about the sophistication of business leaders in HR-related areas and in traditional business disciplines.

The average ratings are shown on a 5-point scale. The use of sound principles in the human resource areas was rated about 3, or at the midpoint of a 5-point scale, whereas their ratings regarding traditional management disciplines were higher, particularly for the disciplines of business strategy and finance. One message is that business leaders are aware that they are less sophisticated when it comes to the principles of human capital.

Table I-1 also shows the correlation between the sophistication ratings and a separate rating of the strength of HR as a strategic partner. The correlations show a significant positive association between the strategic role of HR and the executives' sophistication in the human capital disciplines. In contrast, there is little relationship

TABLE I-1

Business leader sophistication in HR principles

To what extent do your business leaders use sound principles when making decisions about each of the areas below? (1 = little or no extent ... 5 = very great extent)	Average	Correlation with HR's strategic role
Disciplines related to human resources		
Motivation	3.0	0.40
Development and learning	3.0	0.48
Labor markets	3.1	0.33
Culture	3.1	0.32
Organization design	3.1	0.60
More traditional management disciplines		
Business strategy	3.7	0.15
Finance	4.1	−0.04
Marketing	3.2	0.25
Technology	3.3	0.25

Source: Adapted from Edward Lawler and John Boudreau, *Achieving Excellence in Human Resources Management* (Palo Alto, CA: Stanford University Press, 2009).

between the leaders' sophistication in traditional management disciplines and the strategic role of HR. Thus, it isn't that more sophistication in any area correlates with stronger strategic HR functions. Rather, HR is a stronger strategic partner when non-HR leaders use sound principles in the people-related areas.

Retooling Improves the Use of HR Metrics and Analytics

HR leaders are constantly admonished to enhance their analytical skills, and analytical capability is now a common element of most

HR competency systems. By "HR analytics," HR leaders often mean "proving that HR investments are associated with financial outcomes." This purpose is important, but proving that HR programs pay off may not give HR stakeholders the information they need to decide whether those investments will work for them or how they can enhance the effectiveness of those investments by the decisions they make. HR data analysts can draw on logical models, such as portfolio theory, the supply chain, and customer segmentation, to recast their analyses in a more familiar and accepted way.

An impactful measurement system requires not only measures but also a mental model that is acceptable to the audience.[6] Trying to foist complex social statistics analyses on business leaders is a recipe for frustration, and yet these same leaders routinely accept and use sophisticated statistics supporting supply-chain, portfolio, engineering, and marketing frameworks. HR analysts must consider not only the sophistication of the frameworks used within HR but also their accessibility to those outside HR.

As this book shows, the raw materials for a more analytically sophisticated approach are often available in current HR data and measurement systems, but there are untapped opportunities to connect them to proven business frameworks. Retooling HR will enhance the quality of your HR measures and analysis, but its larger effect may be to make them more accessible to their ultimate audience—organizational decision makers—and to hold those decision makers more accountable for what the measures show.

What This Book Does

Each chapter of this book describes how HR can retool a common talent and human capital issue by reframing it in the language of a proven business framework. The HR topics include vital areas such as leadership, incentives, talent acquisition, talent development, and performance management. These reframed perspectives often reveal insights into human capital that go unseen using typical approaches. Thus, the retooled HR frameworks in each chapter are designed to be helpful in themselves, by encouraging HR and non-HR leaders and employees to bring the power of proven business models to bear on vital talent issues.

However, the examples also serve a larger purpose: to encourage HR leaders and their constituents to develop their own enhanced mental models of talent and human capital decisions. The examples show how to make organizations smarter about human capital so that HR leaders and their constituents can begin to develop other applications by drawing on other proven business models or by applying proven business concepts to other HR areas.

You will learn how to address your own talent issues by using logical analysis from proven disciplines. You will understand more clearly that talent issues do not always require learning a completely new language but that the existing business language applies to human capital decisions, and using it can uncover new insights.

HR Leaders Will Be Better Business Partners

If you are an HR leader, this book will help you tackle the perennially elusive role of strategic partner. The roadblock to strategic partnership is often to align human capital issues with the considerations of leaders outside the HR profession. The typical answer has been to suggest that you, the HR leader, become more familiar with the business. This book helps you do that, but in a unique way. When you prepare to describe the connection between your HR deliverables and business outcomes, this book encourages you to step back and consider how your audience already thinks about those connections. Then use those approaches to reframe your analysis. Not only will you know the business better, but also you will use that knowledge to connect better to your constituents.

A Word to Non-HR Business Executives

If you are an HR stakeholder outside the HR profession, this book will help you make better decisions about human capital. Often, your well-intended decisions about people can be improved. That's because the relevance and full impact of your decisions may be obscured by the way HR information is analyzed and presented. Retooling HR will help you better apply your existing expertise to vital talent issues.

HR investments and workforce issues have remarkable parallels with logical frameworks you know well and apply to other resources. Your understanding of frameworks—such as market segmentation, net present value, supply chain, inventory optimization, and risk diversification—gives you a common language to help you work effectively with your counterparts in finance, engineering, operations, and marketing. In the same way, your work with the professionals in your HR organization will be even more productive as you develop a common language to drive decisions about talent.

A Few Cautionary Notes

This book encourages HR leaders and their stakeholders to think in new ways. The business tools described in this book are often many decades old, but applying them to HR decisions is a new idea. HR information systems do not yet contain the data to fully populate the frameworks. Many HR reporting systems do not yet routinely present information in this way. Keep in mind that other established business tools, such as market segmentation and

supply-chain analysis, were not always as data rich and well artic-
ulated as they are now. They all began as proposed models for
which data didn't exist or had not been used in the new way.

Retooling is less about fitting in with current data and more
about expanding current logic. Even without data, the logical
analyses presented here allow leaders to see the impact of relationships they may not yet have considered. Perhaps most important,
even without data, casting talent analytics and decisions in frameworks that already provide deep and important insights about
resources like money, materials, and customers will let executives
see how much better their talent decisions can be and to garner
support for the investments in systems and data that will improve
these decisions even further.

Retooling is first about changing the conversations you have
about talent. Those enhanced conversations will reveal the value
of gathering new data or reporting the data in new ways.

Finally, the business tools described here are part of the basic
lexicon of organizations. In their fully developed form, they are
rich and analytically detailed. Using the ideas presented here, you
should engage your own organization's experts in those business
disciplines. You will find that the models contain a great deal more
depth than this book describes. This book introduces HR leaders
and their stakeholders to the power of applying proven business
tools to human capital, so it draws on the classic versions, because
they are most familiar. As you and your HR leaders apply the
basics, you can seek out experts in these disciplines and apply the
full sophistication of these business tools to talent decisions. That
is the beginning of the path toward a sophisticated HR partnership with other business disciplines.

Finally, keep in mind that talent and human capital are embedded in real people, and you can't manage people with the same
control that you can manage inanimate objects like inventory,
product components, and technology. This book's examples and

implications often describe how to better understand optimal patterns in staffing, career paths, development programs, reward choices, and attrition patterns. Of course, these processes depend on the choices people make, and human behavior is complex. Pipelines and inventory units don't form their own opinions and reactions to the systems that manage them.

Still, that is no reason to ignore the value of proven business tools to identify optimal patterns. Human behavior is complex, but it is not random. Consumer behavior is also subject to human complexity, and yet marketing has long applied analytical frameworks to consumer behavior, with great benefit. Using logical models to reveal how to optimize human capital isn't inconsistent with human complexity. Indeed, if you want to avoid pursuing the wrong goals in a complex and uncertain world, it is essential to employ tools that reveal optimal possibilities clearly.

Book Plan

Chapters 1 through 5 follow the same pattern. First, I identify a common and important human resource dilemma or decision. Second, I describe current HR tools for addressing that dilemma. Third, I show how the dilemma resembles a situation from a proven business discipline and explain how the business discipline typically approaches the issue. Fourth, I show how retooling the HR dilemma using the proven business framework reveals deeper insights, closer connections between HR leaders and their stakeholders, and ways to increase understanding and accountability. Fifth, I suggest steps that HR leaders and their stakeholders can take to begin applying the retooled approaches.

Chapter 1 starts with the most fundamental question: what makes work valuable? It recasts work performance analysis in the framework of engineering performance optimization, thereby focusing on return on improved performance (ROIP). Engineering focuses on how the performance of any element of a system affects the success of the entire system. Work analysis systems (job descriptions, competencies, etc.) can be even more valuable by focusing not only on those jobs or work performance components that are important but also on those that are pivotal. This chapter shows how HR and its stakeholders can better understand where improving the quality or quantity of human capital makes the biggest difference to vital organization outcomes.

Chapter 2 recasts strategic workforce planning as optimizing talent assets against an uncertain future. Scenario planning and portfolio diversification tools from the finance discipline reveal insights by changing the focus from the right talent for the future to optimizing talent against future risks. For purposes of portfolio diversification, HR tools such as competencies, skills, engagement, and deployment can be seen as asset classes. No given asset will fit every future scenario, but portfolio diversification tools can reveal powerful combinations that optimize risk and return. HR and its stakeholders can shift from being risk reducers to being risk optimizers.

Chapter 3 turns to the supply side of strategic workforce planning. How much talent will you have, and how can you influence who joins, stays, moves, and leaves? Which of your employees should get unique deals, and what should be the same for everyone? Which employment features motivate employees most? This chapter recasts the "employment deal" as an application of consumer research and product optimization. Concepts like market segmentation, consumer preferences, and customer purchasing behavior reveal new connections between the employment deal and individual decisions to join, stay, and perform. They show how marketing tools can tap workforce preferences and can use them to optimize the employment deal for various employee and applicant segments.

Chapters 4 and 5 show how operations management and engineering principles can reveal the synergy among HR practices such as staffing, training, rewards, leadership development, and career management. Like the pathways that inventory follows in a supply chain, these practices can be thought of as pathways that talent follows as people develop over time.

Chapter 4 recasts human capital processes as inventory optimization. Employee shortages, surpluses, and vacancies are not simply defects to be minimized but factors to be optimized based on risk, cost, and return. Inventory optimization can show HR leaders and stakeholders how to approach turnover rates, hiring levels, and workforce shortages and surpluses as integrated elements in achieving the needed inventory of talent quality and quantity at the right time and cost. Assumptions—that lower turnover is always better or that filling requisitions as fast as possible is always optimal—are as risky when it comes to human capital as they are when it comes to raw materials or finished goods.

Chapter 5 tackles the question of how to optimize synergy among HR processes in the talent life cycle. Supply-chain concepts and tools can reveal untapped synergy between talent pipeline elements such as recruitment, hiring, training, career movement, and separation. They can be seen as an integrated series of transformations, just as in a supply-chain or manufacturing process.

Chapter 5 takes this even further, focusing on how organizations can optimally combine *multiple* talent pipelines by using the same tools that allow logistics planners and others to combine pipelines—tools such as external and internal design, manufacturing, shipping routes, and supplier networks—with trade-offs in cost, quality, and risk. Should you make or buy talent, and in what positions? Which development experiences should you offer or require, and when? Should business-unit leaders be allowed to hire talent from outside or be required always to use internal candidates? HR tools such as succession and learning management systems have untapped potential to be used to analyze and optimize the routes to success within the organization. More important, decisions about the talent supply chain are often made without full insight into how the complete system works. Without a more comprehensive model, HR and business leaders risk making well-meaning decisions that optimize one part of the system at the expense of other parts.

Finally, chapter 6 presents a conclusion and a call to action for HR leaders to begin building this new set of tools in their own organizations through partnerships between HR and non-HR leaders as well as academics and consultants. It takes up the broader question of strategic workforce planning, showing how the examples suggest an augmented planning concept with implications for measurement, HR strategic partnership, and future HR roles.

1

Using Performance Optimization to Retool Work Analysis

From Job Descriptions, Competencies,

and KPIs to Return on

Improved Performance

This chapter asks a fundamental question: how do you define and optimize work performance? It deals with the sophisticated work analysis and performance systems that HR uses to analyze jobs, map work requirements, and assess required competencies, skills, and abilities. These systems have two vital purposes: to create comprehensive descriptions and identify key performance indicators for work elements (such as jobs, tasks, roles, competencies, skills, and abilities).

Yet hidden within these HR tools is an untapped ability to answer a different question: where would *improving* performance make the greatest difference? This question is faced by employees choosing where to improve their performance, leaders choosing where to set goals and performance incentives, and organizations choosing how to allocate limited human capital investments from where they have less effect to where the effect is greater. Lacking a more sophisticated framework, the answer is often assumed to be that all performance is important and should be maximized. Yet that's like saying every product component must be at maximum quality or that every quality variation must be reduced to zero. When we see it that way, we realize that proven business tools both define performance and optimize performance improvement, and that those same tools can retool HR to identify the *return on improved performance* (ROIP) in the workforce.

How to Focus on the Right Performance

Everyone in an organization must decide where improving work performance makes the greatest difference to success. Every day, managers, supervisors, employees, and leaders make decisions to work on some areas more than others. They set goals that lead to more effort on some things than others, they allocate informal and formal rewards to different tasks, and they decide how to spend their limited time improving some work elements (such as jobs, tasks, roles, competencies, or performance factors). Which work elements should get more attention? Are you confident that this question gets answered correctly across the thousands of decisions that get made every day? How are the choices made?

One way is to assume that all work elements are equally vital, because if they weren't they wouldn't exist in the organization. In the same way, every part of a supply chain, manufacturing process, or product is important, or it wouldn't be there. Yet you don't pay equal attention to every part of a supply chain, process, or product. Asking, "What's important?" doesn't help when you can't pay full attention to everything.

A second approach might be to rank jobs, roles, competencies, or performance elements according what is "key" or "vital." Often, work elements are deemed key because they take a lot of time, are done by lots of people, affect lots of customers or stakeholders, or are in highly paid positions. This definition can also miss something important. At Disneyland, the park cleaners spend most of their time cleaning the park, but they may make their greatest difference to customers when they stop sweeping and answer a guest's question in an amusing and helpful way. It is important that Disneyland ride design engineers meet high standards in their design engineering capability, but they may make their greatest difference when they invent a song like "It's a Small World."[1]

A third approach might be to play to your strengths, focusing on those work areas where employees are strongest and have demonstrated the ability to excel. Yet improving a weak area may make a greater difference. In the U.S. military, soldiers are hired, developed, and rewarded for their ability to carry out traditional combat activities. These are their strengths. However, given that the dominant conflicts are with insurgents, soldiers may make their greatest difference through diplomacy, cultural sensitivity, and restraint. Commanders may make their greatest contribution by observing, rewarding, and developing these nontraditional areas than the traditional war-fighting work elements.

Leaders confront the question of where performance makes the greatest difference when they implement forced-distribution performance systems, such as the 70-20-10 system that Jack Welch made famous at GE. In such a system, managers must identify

20 percent as top performers, 70 percent as middle performers, and 10 percent as bottom performers in each role or job and then remove or improve the bottom 10 percent. Is removing or improving the bottom 10 percent valuable in all cases? Certainly in some situations even the bottom 10 percent are doing an adequate job and are doing better than those who could be hired or promoted. By definition, continually removing or improving the bottom 10 percent will make the bottom 10 percent more similar to the middle 70 percent and thus make removing the bottom 10 percent less effective in improving workforce quality. Traditional work and performance systems don't quite answer the question of where a 70-20-10 approach is helpful and where it is harmful.

This question also goes to the heart of goal setting. On which aspects of a job should managers set aggressive goals for employees, and on which aspects should they encourage meeting adequate standards but not more? If employees are striving for excellence where it doesn't matter and accepting adequate performance where excellence would pay off, that's a problem. Yet does it really make sense for leaders to approach goal setting by striving for excellence on everything? If every work element makes an equal contribution, then employees can be good performers by pursuing any combination of work outcomes. Yet some work outcomes almost always make a greater difference and deserve the greater focus.

In performance management and goal setting, the full effect of decisions is often obscured, and so poor decisions can be made. Well-meaning leaders want to drive performance where it matters most. They are often held accountable for the decisions they make about giving informal recognition, evaluating performance, setting goals, and knowing when performance goals need to change with a changing mission. However, this kind of performance differentiation requires insight into what matters most, and more time and energy to explain and motivate the proper performance. Lacking a framework for logically focusing where it matters most, leaders understandably often give equal weight to everything or give moderate evaluations and rewards to everyone.

This practice minimizes disruption and gives employees a sense of equality and fairness. It may not even seriously reduce performance in the short term. However, HR leaders and others are often held accountable for related goals, such as investing in performance improvement and rewards where it matters most and uncovering those work elements or talent segments where improved performance has the greatest impact on organization success. When unit leaders don't own the full consequences of their decisions, it is understandable that they are reluctant or unable to make hard decisions about which aspect of performance matters and how best to allocate limited resources. They can be forgiven for avoiding controversy, when that is what they experience most vividly, yet the hidden consequences of such behavior can be extremely harmful.

Engineering has faced this kind of question for a long time. Leaders of manufacturing, product design, distribution, sales, or service are held accountable not for improving everything but for finding out where performance improvement makes the greatest difference. The tools used by engineers and others to define that question and help stakeholders make better decisions can show HR leaders how they can retool their typical approach to work analysis and performance management and engage HR stakeholders in focusing on the work performance and talent characteristics that matter most.

HR Tools: Descriptions and Inventories

HR tools to define and describe work and performance cover everything from tasks, to skills, to competencies, to typical career interests. At the most basic level are *job descriptions* and *specifications* that catalogue work elements and categorize them into jobs, often measuring the amount of time spent on each element. *Competency* systems define capabilities that span multiple jobs and positions (such as vision, focus, action orientation, and ethics) and often provide a common language for training, performance, staffing, and other HR processes. *Performance management* systems translate strategy into goals and key performance indicators (KPIs).

Can the language that describes the work be retooled to answer the question posed earlier: Where does improved performance make the greatest difference? That requires improving the connection between work analysis and business outcomes and extending the emphasis from describing work elements to finding which work elements matter most.

Boeing, Airbus, and the Talent Challenges of New-Age Aircraft Production

On December 15, 2009, Boeing's 787 Dreamliner made its first flight, marking a success that was preceded by two years of delays and a $2.6 billion write-down because of problems. The first flight had been set for June 2009, but a design flaw associated with components connecting the wings and the fuselage delayed the flight and took almost six months to fix and test.

When Boeing tackled the creation of the 787 Dreamliner, it undertook at least two significant strategic challenges. One was to build the aircraft out of composites rather than the traditional aluminum. The other was to share the design tasks, financial risks, and financial returns with a far-flung set of supply-chain partners. To reduce the multi-billion dollar development cost, Boeing authorized its suppliers to design and build major aircraft components that Boeing would then assemble. Boeing worked with partners in countries as diverse as France, Italy, Japan, Korea, and China, in part because countries where Boeing has significant production capacity also purchase more Boeing aircraft (Chinese airlines had ordered sixty of the new jets as of January 2006). Figure 1-1 shows the extent of Boeing's global supplier network.

This approach was very different from the one Boeing had traditionally pursued with its highly successful earlier commercial aircraft models such as the 747 and 767. In the past, Boeing shouldered the design tasks itself, delivering precise specifications to its suppliers, and then monitored the quality and cost of the suppliers' products

FIGURE 1-1

Boeing 787 global suppliers

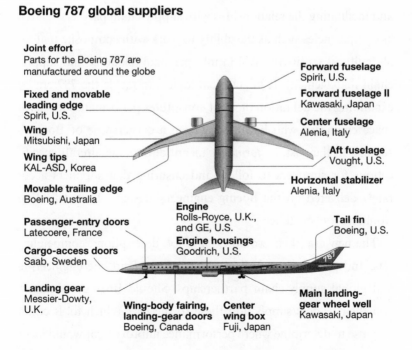

Joint effort
Parts for the Boeing 787 are manufactured around the globe

Fixed and movable leading edge
Spirit, U.S.

Wing
Mitsubishi, Japan

Wing tips
KAL-ASD, Korea

Movable trailing edge
Boeing, Australia

Passenger-entry doors
Latecoere, France

Cargo-access doors
Saab, Sweden

Landing gear
Messier-Dowty, U.K.

Engine
Rolls-Royce, U.K., and GE, U.S.

Engine housings
Goodrich, U.S.

Wing-body fairing, landing-gear doors
Boeing, Canada

Center wing box
Fuji, Japan

Forward fuselage
Spirit, U.S.

Forward fuselage II
Kawasaki, Japan

Center fuselage
Alenia, Italy

Aft fuselage
Vought, U.S.

Horizontal stabilizer
Alenia, Italy

Tail fin
Boeing, U.S.

Main landing-gear wheel well
Kawasaki, Japan

Source: J. L. Lunsford, "Boeing Scrambles to Repair Problems with New Plane," *Wall Street Journal*, December 7, 2007, A1, A13.

against these specifications.[2] In the 787 era, Boeing would invite its suppliers to share the design tasks, along with the risks and returns of producing the 787 on time and on budget. Boeing pursued global sourcing through an extended network of relationships, a practice that required transparency, communication, trust, and genuine reciprocity as the relationships shifted from adversarial to collaborative, from procurement to partnership.[3] Airbus chief executive Tom Enders, commenting on the 787's first flight, spoke from experience, saying, "Flying was the simplest part, the hard part was the complexity of industrialization."[4]

Strategic HR dictated that these challenges be reflected in the design of the work and the definition of work performance. Doing so might involve recasting Boeing's job descriptions, competencies, and key performance indicators. Boeing might, for example, add to the role of aerospace engineer the tasks of composite engineering and facilitating the relationships with supply-chain partners, as well as competencies such as the ability to work with composite materials, cultural sensitivity, skill in interpersonal relations, and supply-chain management. It might seem logical to tackle the 787 era by expanding the definition of what constitutes performance for aerospace engineers, who had always been a cornerstone of Boeing's success. In the past, *performance* meant developing aircraft specifications for suppliers to follow and ensuring that suppliers accurately delivered on the Boeing engineers' designs. That definition would no longer suffice.

The new era, then, would expand job descriptions, competency sets, and performance indicators to reflect composite engineering and global supply-chain partnerships. Should Boeing's engineers and their leaders simply add these to the list? Which tools could they use to determine where performance improvement would most improve organization goals? Although the Boeing engineers would increasingly work with new materials and with new partners, the time spent on traditional engineering would still be substantial. Enhancing the new competencies therefore could be valuable, but should the company invest less in traditional competencies to make that happen? Well-meaning leaders and engineers would make those choices, but they might well make a wrong decision if armed only with lists of competencies and performance indicators.

An even more important question took this concern up a level. Were Boeing's engineers the right choice for enhancing the global supply chain? Having engineers who were better at facilitating global supply-chain teams was certainly consistent with the company's strategy. Smart engineers and their leaders, focusing on engineering performance, would logically see better performance in this area as a good thing. But was engineer performance the *most effective* way to achieve supply-chain cooperation and integration? Were engineers really the key pivot point in ensuring cooperation and integration?

The perspective that was needed to answer this question lay outside the engineering role. Often, it is HR leaders who have this kind of perspective. The challenge for Boeing was to find a tool that would identify the places where performance improvements would be most valuable. Armed with that insight, HR leaders and stakeholders would be able to make better decisions about what to emphasize.

Reframing Work Performance Using an Engineering Perspective

The question facing Boeing was not only which competencies and performance elements should be added to the engineering position, but where improving performance would make the greatest difference in the firm's strategic success. This "performance tolerance" question has long been addressed in engineering. Indeed it was while working with engineers in several companies to uncover the talent implications of their strategies that my colleagues and I wrestled with the question of whether enhancing some jobs or performance elements might be more valuable than enhancing others.

The engineers in these companies struggled with this question because they had always approached work performance using tools such as job descriptions, competency models, and KPIs. They tended to interpret these tools as suggesting that all the elements of performance were vital and equally valuable. If something wasn't important, it wouldn't be in the job description, right? Yet in their daily work, they could see that the difference in performance between their best and average engineers in motivating teams and coordinating across projects had a much greater impact than the difference between their best and worst engineers at technical specifications—even though both were important, and both were in the job description.

At one organization, as we were discussing the issue, one of the engineers had an "Aha!" moment. "Wait!" he said. "This is not a new concept. We do this all the time. When we have a component of a product or software program that we know can operate within wide tolerances, we don't try to make it overly precise. We allow the wide tolerance, because it doesn't do any harm. On the other hand, when a component causes big problems if it deviates even a little, we pay much more attention to keeping that component within standards. Every component is *important*, but *improving* the quality of every component is not equally valuable."

The dilemma of how to unearth vital pivot points among system components is not unique to HR. Every management discipline has systems that describe the basic components of their resource, processes, or products. Engineering describes components of everything from cell phones to computers to bridges in common terms such as size, tolerances, costs, and chemical makeup. Marketing describes advertisements in terms of themes, length, music, and so on. Manufacturing describes machines in terms of speed, capacity, performance variation, and maintenance.

However, armed only with such lists of components, decision makers in these areas would face the same dilemma that they face with work analysis. It is one thing to know the components, but that alone does not show how to most significantly improve product performance, manufacturing efficiency, and goals. The term *return on improved performance* (ROIP) captures the idea of optimal investment. Like *return on investment* (ROI), return on improved performance focuses on the change in value associated with a change in performance. This chapter focuses on improvements in performance quality, but note that the same idea also applies to improvements in performance *quantity*. Often, the pivot point is the difference in the number of people available, when having vacancies or not can significantly affect success. In most cases a combination of quality and quantity defines pivot points.

Three Engineering Tools to Measure ROIP in HR

Three tools used in other business disciplines illustrate how to analyze and measure ROIP: Kano analysis, risk–value analysis, and process constraint (or bottleneck) analysis.

Kano Analysis

Kano analysis, named after Noriaki Kano, who coined the term in the 1980s, shows how improved performance has widely differing effects.[5] Figure 1-2 shows the various curves.

Here, Kano analysis shows the range of consumer reactions to product or service features. The "Excitement" curve reflects high

FIGURE 1-2

Kano analysis applied to product or service features

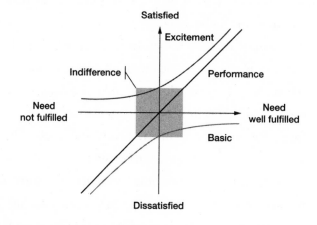

Source: http://upload.wikimedia.org/wikipedia/commons/1/14/Kano_Model.gif.

value placed on high performance but little disappointment placed on low performance. Consumers experience this excitement, for example, when they receive a discount they didn't expect. They are excited to get the discount, but because they didn't expect it, they would not have been dissatisfied without it.

The "Performance" curve reflects a different reaction: when the value placed on higher performance offsets the value of lower performance; an example is price, where a dollar higher offsets a dollar lower. The "Basic" curve shows the situation when a product's performance must meet a minimum standard; missing the standard does great harm, but going beyond the standard adds little value. An example of basic performance is the timing of required tax reports. On-time performance is necessary; there is little value in filing them early but great harm in filing them late.

It is not always possible to estimate these curves with numbers, but the logic provides valuable insights in marketing, engineering, and product design—and potentially in HR.

Applying Kano Analysis to Boeing's 787 Strategy

Figures 1-3 and 1-4 apply the Kano concept to two of the relevant work elements of a Boeing aerospace engineer: technical engineering and facilitation of global supplier teams.

Figure 1-3 shows the engineer job before the 787 era. The significant contribution is developing precise specifications for airplane

FIGURE 1-3

Kano analysis applied to the traditional aerospace engineer job

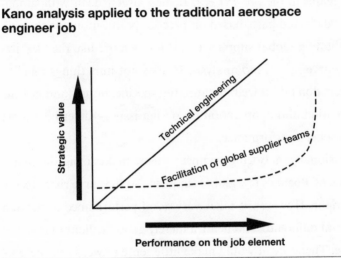

FIGURE 1-4

Kano analysis applied to the 787-era aerospace engineer job

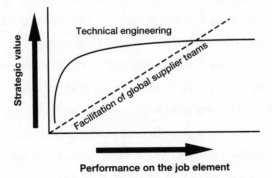

components and assigning those specifications to internal or external production teams. The ROIP of technical engineering has the shape of a "Performance" attribute in Kano analysis. In Boeing's traditional processes, better engineering is increasingly valuable, and poorer engineering offsets that better value. Thus, in the traditional strategy, it made sense for Boeing to continually improve engineering.

The dotted line in figure 1-3 represents the ROIP for facilitating global teams in the pre-787 era. Boeing largely dealt with suppliers that delivered parts based on precise specifications, so the skill of facilitating global supplier teams looks more like the "Excitement" curve in a Kano analysis. It does not hurt things much if engineers don't do it well, because the specifications—and not the coordination and cooperation on design issues—determine most of a supplier's performance.

Occasionally, a Boeing engineer might make a big difference with one of Boeing's few global suppliers, so the curve rises steeply at the right. However, it takes very good performance to make a significant difference, and being a merely good facilitator is usually just fine. Therefore, it would make little sense to weed out the bottom 10 percent of facilitators. Engineers who are not very good at facilitation do little harm, and in the traditional situation it takes a lot of effort to improve their facilitation to a level where it creates high value. Engineers and their leaders who grew up in the traditional era have become accustomed to focusing on technical engineering and much less on supplier facilitation.

Figure 1-4 shows the same analysis for the role of aerospace engineer in the 787 era. Now these workers share the product and manufacturing design tasks with supplier teams, whose members may often know more than Boeing's engineers do about composite construction and clearly are more knowledgeable about the suppliers' design and manufacturing capabilities.

In the 787 era, the ROIP for technical engineering, shown in figure 1-3 as the solid line, is more of a "Basic" attribute in Kano analysis. It is important that it be done at a high standard, and it is harmful if engineers do it poorly; but when it comes to the 787, which relies much more on the design expertise of the supply chain, the value of engineer performance on technical engineering levels off above the required standard. The dotted line shows the ROIP for facilitation of global supplier teams in the 787 era, with suppliers as design partners. The ROIP on this work element now is shaped like a "Performance" attribute in Kano analysis. Improvements are more valuable than before, because the new strategy relies a great deal on this element and because the difference in engineer quality is likely much greater than for traditional engineering.

Contrast the results of Kano analysis with those of typical work analysis and performance management based on job descriptions: competencies or even KPIs would usually reflect both technical engineering and supplier facilitation but give us little guidance on the shape of the curves. It is the shape of the curve that is the key to the evolution of the aerospace engineer role. The shape of the ROIP curve is the element that allows engineers and their leaders to understand the connection between the larger strategy and their decisions about where to improve performance. If leaders are to be held accountable for being strategic in their performance management, then HR leaders need to provide them with tools, such as Kano analysis, to make this connection.

Kano analysis shows us that under the new strategy for the 787 era, engineers must break old habits. Rather than simply strive for the highest possible technical engineering and "good enough" supplier facilitation, they should set their goal to produce outstanding engineering enabled by the highest possible facilitation. All the tools of HR apply here, but by adding the engineering curves, you can improve your analytical logic and engagement with stakeholders by revealing the connection between HR strategy and the company's overall strategy, in a language they already trust and understand.

Combining Risk with Performance-Value Analysis

The ROIP idea, combined with the concept of risk optimization, answers questions like, "Where should I be willing to tolerate wide performance variation, in hopes that the high end will make up for the low end?" "Where should I reduce performance variation to mitigate the downside risk of bad performance, even if I give up some of the upside?" Engineering deals with these kinds of questions all the time in a process known as *risk–value analysis*.[6] Commercial airlines tolerate wide variation in the age and wear of the interior appointments of aircraft, but they would ground a flight immediately if diagnostics indicated even a small possibility that a component of the engine is slightly out of specification. Passengers will tolerate a certain amount of age and superficial wear, but the consequences of a bad engine are too serious to allow use of the aircraft.

From an engineering perspective, the decision to ground planes for a malfunctioning engine light, but not to do so for worn seat backs, is the same logical idea behind HR performance systems that stipulate where to remove or improve the bottom 10 percent as a way to reduce job performance variation. Organizations would not apply a blanket policy of grounding aircraft whenever any component is at the bottom 10 percent of its tolerance level. In the same way the value of removing or improving the bottom 10 percent of workers depends on the consequences of performance variation and risk.

Applying Risk–Value Analysis to Boeing Engineering Performance

This idea shows up for Boeing when we consider the ROIP curve for technical engineering, comparing the pre-787 and post-787 eras. Figure 1-5 shows the two curves for technical engineering from the earlier figures.

Because the ROIP curve for technical engineering is flatter in the 787 era than it was in the pre-787 era, Boeing would much prefer the narrow distribution of performance shown in the dotted-line bell curve shown at the bottom in figure 1-5. A wide distribution, shown in the solid-line bell curve at the bottom, entails a greater chance of very good performance but also a greater chance of poor performance. In the 787 era, good performance on technical engineering doesn't offset poor performance as it did in the pre-787 era, when superlative engineering design was more significantly related to success. In the pre-787 era, the wider curve was better, because high performance would offset low performance, but in the 787 era,

FIGURE 1-5

Risk–value analysis of technical engineering at Boeing

Narrow risk distribution is better in the 787 era than in the pre-787 era

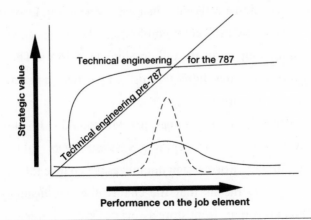

a more tightly controlled and narrow range of engineering performance is better.

How Risk–Value Analysis Explains the McDonald's Versus the Starbucks Front Line

Consider the role of a barista at Starbucks, and the similar role of counter service associate at McDonald's. Both roles involve preparing the product, interacting with customers, taking payments, working with the team, good attendance, and good job performance. The description for these roles might look similar at both Starbucks and McDonald's. But risk–value analysis reveals hidden and important strategic differences.

McDonald's and Starbucks choose to compete differently. McDonald's is known for consistency and speed. Its stores automate many of the key tasks of food preparation, customer interaction, and team roles. Each McDonald's product has an assigned number so that associates need only press the number on the register to record the customer order. Indeed, it is not unusual to hear customers themselves ordering by saying, "I'll take a number three with a Coke, and supersize it."

At one point McDonald's even had the drive-up ordering receiver connected to a call center in a remote location. Drive-up orders were taken by call center employees, who had been specially trained in drive-up etiquette and upselling techniques. This meant that in-store associates didn't take drive-up orders, a practice that further focused their roles.[7]

This is likely a good strategy for McDonald's. It allows the company to acquire and deploy a vast variety of talent in its stores, because the work design minimizes the chance for mistakes. However, it also means that the chance for significant performance breakthroughs from store associates is also lower.

Contrast that with Starbucks. Starbucks baristas are a highly diverse and often multitalented group. The allure of Starbucks as a "third place" (home, work, and Starbucks) is predicated in part on the possibility of interesting interactions with Starbucks baristas. Blogs, Tweets, and Facebook pages are devoted to the Starbucks baristas. Some of them are opera singers and actually sing out the orders. Their personal styles are clearly on display and range from Gothic to country to hipster. There are few online pages devoted to McDonald's associates. Starbucks counts on that diversity as part of its image.[8] This means that it needs to give its baristas wide latitude to sing, joke, and kibitz with customers. Starbucks may not be able to tap as wide an array of possible talent as McDonald's, because there is more room for error at Starbucks. Starbucks may have to spend more on evaluating applicant and new-hire quality. However, that additional quality control in hiring, and the room for error in job performance, is the price that Starbucks pays to gain the opportunity to have interesting baristas.

The various elements of job descriptions, and even competencies, of Starbucks baristas are similar to those of McDonald's counter associates. Both would list tasks such as preparing the product, interacting with customers, and using the equipment. Leaders and associates who treated all the elements as equally important would achieve moderately good performance. However, the strategic decisions by McDonald's and Starbucks lead to vastly different payoffs (and risks) from these work elements and gain the potential for significant strategic advantage. Figure 1-6 shows the risk–return analysis described earlier applied here to the two restaurants.

On the left in figure 1-6 is McDonald's classic risk-averse approach to performance. McDonald's designs the work to maintain a tight distribution. McDonald's guards against poor performance

FIGURE 1-6

Risk–value analysis for frontline jobs: McDonald's versus Starbucks

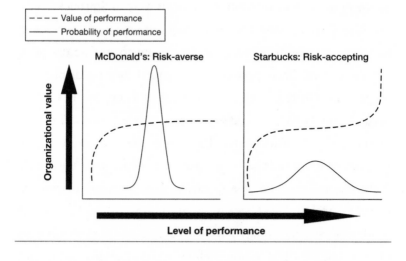

by restricting the performance range, because its strategy does not require highly creative service on the high end of the performance scale. McDonald's wants high performance on the job, but "high" is defined within a narrow range.

On the right is the Starbucks combination of risk aversion on the low end of performance and risk seeking on the high end of performance. Starbucks accepts and even encourages a wide array of performance levels (shown by the wider distribution curve), because the way it competes creates a high payoff from an extraordinary innovation on the right side. Starbucks also wants to guard against poor performance on the left, but if it wants the high end, it must accept some risk at the low end. For example, some customers may be annoyed if the opera singer gets too boisterous, but Starbucks can't simply say, "No singing" as McDonald's can. Starbucks must allow singing to have the chance of creating customer delight on the right side of the performance curve.

Constraint (Bottleneck) Analysis

A final method of discovering ROIP is a hallmark of operations management. *Constraint, or bottleneck, analysis* identifies where improving the performance of interrelated processes will make the greatest difference. The basic principle is that when several processes depend on each other, improving performance at the constraint will most improve the entire process. In an assembly line, all the machines are important, but if you want to most improve the capacity of the system, you raise the capacity of the machine that is the bottleneck. Constraint analysis therefore finds those places where the return on improved performance is greatest.

Constraint Analysis and the Pivotal Roles for the Boeing 787. Constraint analysis can be applied to Boeing's 787 strategic need to look beyond engineering performance. This is a good example of how an enhanced framework can give leaders the perspective necessary to see the whole issue, and not only the one in their unit. For the 787, the bottleneck turned out to be the task of facilitating global supplier partners.

The 787-era process looked like this: Boeing provided design specifications, the supplier generated component designs, the supplier produced components for testing, Boeing integrated the components seamlessly into a final aircraft, Boeing tested the aircraft, Boeing worked with the supplier to make necessary changes, and finally the supplier produced the components at sufficient volumes and quality.

The first step of constraint analysis was to answer the question, Where in this process did Boeing's aircraft engineers make the greatest difference? They had a great deal to do with the beginning of the process, because they created the broad design of the aircraft. However, much of the process was embedded in the internal supplier processes of design, testing, manufacturing, delivery, and production. The significant constraints might lie in one or more of these other parts of the process. In that case, were engineers the best workers to address those constraints?

In conversations with Boeing leaders, they emphasized that a surprisingly vital element to achieving their business strategy was the transformation of the job of their own contract managers. Traditionally Boeing's contract managers were heavily engaged in technical and financial auditing, attending to details about whether the supplier delivered highly specific components to the required cost and specifications. Contract managers also were deeply involved in observing and evaluating supplier operations, with the purpose of ensuring that suppliers operated to the specific requirements of the contract or service level agreement.

This work would remain important in the 787 era, but for the strategy to work, the contract manager had a newly extended role. Contract managers were already deeply embedded with supplier organizations, so their capability to facilitate coordination and cooperation with the supplier and to assess supplier technical capabilities in a complex and fast-moving value chain was the key to addressing many of the constraints. Although the 787 strategy had made facilitating supplier relationships more pivotal for Boeing's engineers, company managers began to think that improving this capability among contract managers might be the greatest constraint and thus might offer the greater opportunity.

Not only can ROIP analysis identify *what* the vital work elements are—such as facilitating global supplier relationships for the Boeing 787—but it also can identify *where* such work elements will make the biggest difference in organization success. Pursuing the 787 strategy meant that Boeing would need to get better at working with and coordinating suppliers. The natural tendency was to build that capacity in its engineers, who had always been the lead positions in aircraft design. Using constraint analysis with the ROIP concept revealed that Boeing needed that capability in a position not traditionally thought of as part of the design process: contract managers. Indeed, there might not even be such a "job" at Boeing. A hybrid position might be the answer, one that had the supplier relationship elements of a traditional contract manager, combined with the design and coordination elements of an aerospace engineer.

Gaining more control over the supply chain can also be accomplished by acquiring the human (and other) capital from Boeing's suppliers. In 2009, Boeing spent over one billion dollars in South Carolina alone, acquiring the manufacturing operations of Vought Aircraft Industries and the fuselage factory of Alenia North America.[9] While these decisions are based on many factors, one potential motivation might be that the constraint on the contract manager role makes it more strategically effective for Boeing to manage suppliers as employees rather than contractors.

How HR Leaders Can Use ROIP to Retool

As an HR leader, you're invited by this chapter to consider whether your systems for defining and describing work, performance, and capabilities can do more if you exploit the additional perspective of ROIP. Can systems that currently describe the work be retooled to offer insights into where improving performance makes the greatest difference?

Here's how to find out. Start by looking at the job description, competency set, or KPIs of a vital job. Ask the questions behind Kano analysis. Do some elements of the job have different curves? All elements are important, but does the value of performance in some of them level off at some point? Do others continue to add

The Paradox of 70-20-10 in a World of the Long Tail

The idea that employment is the primary way organizations and their contributors interact is so instinctive that it may blind organizations to an alternative form of engagement. Consider open-source communities of practice, groups of software developers who rely on contributions from thousands or even millions of community members. It is called "open source" because the source code of the software is open and available (and thus can easily be altered) rather than proprietary and unavailable. For example, Linux is an open-source software operating system that relies on the free contributions of its community of developers. They contribute for many reasons, including enhancing their reputation, working for the good of the programming community, gaining the satisfaction of contributing to something they believe in, and so on. For the most part, they are not employees. Keeping them engaged is often less a matter of money than it is the careful nurturing of relationships among the community.

This changes the nature of the ROIP curve. For example, a single person in the community may have the idea that will help Linux avoid being compromised by a hacker. That person may contribute such an idea only every few years, but if she is a motivated part of the community, she will donate it to Linux.

It would be almost impossible for Linux, or any other organization, to manage this kind of performance through traditional employment. No one can afford to have people on the payroll who contribute only one idea every several years, but an open-source community provides precisely the engagement model it requires. Essentially, the performance distribution is one with a long, flat tail of small contributions by almost everyone, but then a spike at the right side, where high performance occurs. A few good ideas that will make or break Linux are contributed by a few people in the community. A similar situation exists in the worldwide effort to map the genetic code of various organisms. There is evidence that the top 0.75 percent of contributors to the genetic sequence database provide more than 17 percent of all the contributions.[a]

Most organizations assume that performance is distributed like a bell curve, and that is the basis for popular notions like dividing the workforce into the top 20 percent, middle 70 percent, and bottom 10 percent. The idea of getting rid of the bottom 10 percent makes sense if you assume they are of little value and can be easily replaced, but it makes less sense if the bottom 10 percent contains the person who doesn't contribute an idea for years, but when she does it will be exactly the idea you need, as in an open-source community. Such a community might do well to welcome everyone and not weed people out. On the other end of the scale, rewarding the top 20 percent makes sense if that group contains the inflection point in the performance curve. However, if it's actually the people in the top 1 percent who make the significant contributions, perhaps the standard should be set even higher. Assumptions like bell curve distributions may mask opportunities that are revealed by a closer look at the ROIP.

a. L. G. Zucker, M. R. Darby, and M. B. Brewer, "Intellectual Human Capital and the Birth of U.S. Biotechnology Enterprises," *American Economic Review* 88, no. 1 (1998): 290–306.

value no matter how high performance gets? Consider sketching some of these curves to see whether you can uncover areas where it might make sense to shift attention from one element to another one that offers a greater payoff.

When you're designing or implementing performance management systems, take the opportunity to use ROIP to better coach leaders and employees on ways to find the vital pivot points where improved performance makes the greatest difference. For example, encourage leaders to consider the relative payoff among the goals they set for employees. Does every performance goal need to be maximized? Is "good enough" sufficient for some job elements? If employees were to achieve a 10 percent higher performance level for each of the key performance elements, would the added value to the organization be the same? If not, where would it be greatest?

HR can also involve business leaders and employees in helping define the ROIP curves. One way is to embed curve drawing into the normal cycle of strategy, performance management, and goal-setting processes.[10] Some HR leaders begin not by drawing the curves, but by asking leaders simply to categorize positions in the organization as to whether performance differences are "definitely highly pivotal," "possibly pivotal," and "important but probably not pivotal."

Most HR systems are not yet set up to calculate and assign numbers to ROIP curves, but the raw materials exist in today's HR systems. Even when the numbers are imperfect, the concepts are engaging to leaders. For example, Alan Eustace, Google's vice president of engineering, told the *Wall Street Journal* that one top-notch engineer is worth three hundred times or more than the average and that he would rather lose an entire incoming class of engineering graduates than one exceptional technologist.[11] Was this estimate based on precise numbers? Probably not. But the insight it reveals regarding where Google will put its emphasis is significant. Recasting performance management to reflect where differences in performance have large impact allows leaders to engage the logic they use for other resources and make educated guesses that can be informative. For example, if a top-notch engineer is worth three hundred times more than an average one, that estimate alone can be used to calculate the return on investment for improved training, selection and rewards to such engineers.[12]

One way to calculate ROIP for various job elements is to relate each element to performance outcomes. Alec Levenson and Tracy Faber used surveys and performance information to look at the return on improved performance among route sales representatives (RSRs) at Frito-Lay. They found that the representatives spent time on three tasks: driving and delivery (loading the products onto the truck properly, driving the route, and unloading the product), selling (having a good relationship with store managers, negotiating for favorable shelf space), and merchandising (placing the product correctly on the shelves, checking for stale product). Using performance data and surveys of RSRs, they found that "even though sales activities take only a fraction of RSRs' time each day . . . sales activities were critical for hiking sales revenue."[13] The ROIP on sales was high even though the time spent was not. Also, the ROIPs of driving and selling differed depending on the type of route: High-volume routes served big-box stores like Walmart, whereas low-volume routes served small-footprint stores like neighborhood convenience markets.

Leaders were asked to rate drivers on their ability to do each of the parts of the job. Then, to calculate ROIP, these ratings were correlated with the sales levels of the RSRs and analyzed by the type of route. They found that "on the low-volume routes, differences in sales task skills were the main influence on sales performance . . . On the high-volume routes, differences in driving and delivery task skills were a stronger differentiator of performance than sales task skills."[14]

Another way to obtain numbers for ROIP is called *utility analysis* in industrial psychology. One utility analysis approach asks employees or leaders to place a value on the performance of someone who is better than 50 percent of performers and someone who is better than 85 percent of performers, with the difference giving an idea of the ROIP on that performance. Other approaches take actual measures of performance on various elements of the job and measure how much they differ among employees.[15]

How Business Leaders Can Use ROIP to Retool

As a leader outside HR, you need to challenge traditional HR systems to help you do more. The idea is to change the conversation from describing the work to focusing on pivot points and identifying where performance improvements pay off. Look beyond performance elements in terms of their importance or what takes a lot of time, and push instead for discussions about where performance makes the greatest difference.

You'll run into the ROIP question when you're evaluating performance, setting goals, and considering where to put your scarce time and effort to improve performance. The first step is to treat work performance as having many elements, just like any product or process. Invite your HR leaders to work with you to help define those elements.

Then require ROIP analysis for work performance just as you would for any other discipline. Identify the bottlenecks in your processes, and ask where improving performance would make the biggest difference in correcting that bottleneck. Work with your HR leaders to answer questions like, "If I could improve only one or two work elements, where should I place my efforts?" Challenge your HR leaders to analyze the information they already have about performance on various work elements, relating it to measures of overall performance (as in the example with Frito-Lay in this chapter). Even if you can't get numbers, don't abandon the idea. Try drawing rough ROIP curves for specific work elements or setting goals that reflect where ROIP levels off and where it rises sharply, as the example of Google discussed earlier.

Finally, when your organization's strategy changes, as with Boeing and the 787, challenge strategic workforce planning to go beyond predicting gaps in headcount needed for today's jobs. Instead, ask, "Where are the significant pivot points in our strategy, and what new performance elements will become more pivotal as a result?"

At Unilever, for example, Peter Attfield, vice president of HR, Global Category, Global Functions and Foodsolutions, describes a process in which leaders used the ROIP idea to analyze leadership allocation. They rated the relative impact of differences in leader performance (essentially the ROIP) in each of their regions, categories, and product lines. The ratings were subjective estimates, but they were done collectively to achieve consensus. Surprisingly, it was not always the largest or traditionally most prestigious region, category, or product line where leadership made the biggest difference. Some smaller and emerging markets had larger ROIP on leadership than more established areas.

Next, Unilever leaders worked with HR to summarize the information on the quality of the individual leaders in each region, category, or product line position. They combined the ROIP estimates with the quality estimates and found that they did not always have the highest-quality leader in the position having the highest leadership ROIP. Although virtually all of the leaders were good performers, the analysis revealed opportunities to better match the highest-quality leaders to the areas where their performance would make the biggest difference.[16]

<hr>

Hidden within the standard job analysis tools of HR is the opportunity to significantly change the way we look at work. You can adapt the proven business tools of Kano analysis, risk–return analysis, and constraint analysis to analyze the work. The result is to revolutionize how organizations analyze, invest, and optimize the return on improved performance at work, just as these tools have revolutionized return on improved performance for manufacturing, engineering, and marketing.

Opportunities to Improve HR

- Use information about jobs, performance, and capabilities to uncover where improving employee performance has the greatest impact on strategic and business success

- Invest in performance management, work analysis and competency systems where they make the greatest improvement

- Understand where forced-distribution performance systems do and do not make sense

- Recast performance management systems to optimize performance risk and return

Opportunities to Improve HR's Connection with Key Stakeholders

- Understand how workforce performance connects to business outcomes the way engineering connects process or component performance to outcomes

- Treat performance improvement for employees like performance improvement in engineering, marketing, or operations

- Analyze the risks of less-than-top performance in the workforce like similar risks in product design and manufacturing

- Use an "80-20 rule" for workforce performance, focusing on the 20 percent of performance that makes 80 percent of the difference

2

Using Portfolio Diversification to Retool Talent Scenarios

From the Right Talent for the Future to
Talent Hedging Against a Risky Future

CEOs often refer to their leadership or talent as a "portfolio," borrowing an idea from financial analysis. They often mean simply that their capabilities fit together. For other resources, however, portfolio optimization goes further, providing a tool to optimize risk and return in the face of an uncertain future. Financial investment systems make this very clear. They require decision makers to explicitly deal with uncertainty, they provide tools to help, and they hold decision makers accountable for the consequences.

This chapter deals with managing risk in strategic workforce planning and human resource management. HR management is often devoted to mitigating risks, such as the risk of lawsuits, accidents, and so on. Yet human capital, like all resources, is not perfectly predictable, so decisions about talent always balance risk against return, even if decision makers don't know it. Particular skills, capabilities, roles, and competencies have different value depending on future situations. Chapter 1 showed how the capability to facilitate global supplier partners was far more pivotal for Boeing in the 787 era, but Boeing's strategic planners also had to decide how heavily to invest in it *before* they could be certain about the 787's success. They were placing a bet in the face of an uncertain future.

Leaders constantly make bets when they invest in asset classes that take time to build and have different payoffs depending on what happens. For example, the decision to build call centers in one or both of two countries means placing a bet on the future volume and cost of call center service in each country. Leaders are accustomed to weighing whether to bet on one country or the other, whether to build generically in a way that will work in both, or whether to build in both countries at a level that best reflects each country's likely growth.

HR leaders and their stakeholders also make choices about investing, but in their case it is investing in talent and organizational capabilities. Whether they realize it or not, their choices can extrapolate from the past, bet on the most probable future, or prepare for multiple future scenarios at once.

Smart and well-meaning HR leaders and stakeholders can miss opportunities if they don't realize they have a choice. Some leaders may stick with past investments, assuming that these investments will work in the future and knowing for certain that this strategy avoids the costs of change. Others may change, often choosing to build talent to fit the one set of future conditions that seems most likely. Still others may build generic talent capabilities, which are valuable no matter what happens, assuming that they are guaranteeing at least some future value. Finally, some may build in agility as a workforce capability, planning to change later when the future is more certain.

The consequences of these decisions are seldom clear until long after they are made. It takes time to build talent capabilities, and the future often changes too quickly to know for certain what talent capabilities to create. Often, HR tools such as strategic workforce planning systems, competency and capability assessments, and scenario analysis identify one future and help leaders identify the most significant talent gaps and necessary workforce investments to fill those gaps. That's an important capability, just as it's important that financial systems show leaders which assets fit a particular future investment climate. However, this approach raises the question of whether leaders chose the right bet and whether it would have been better to invest in an alternative or in several at once. Similarly, it's important for strategic workforce planning to be able to project gaps and investments that reflect a particular future scenario, but it's also important for such systems to help leaders make the right talent bets when faced with multiple possible future scenarios.

Talent decision makers can be more adept and accountable for managing workforce risk. This approach requires HR methods that explicitly optimize talent implications and the probabilities of multiple future scenarios. Portfolio theory provides a language and logic to make HR and its stakeholders better at considering risk, return, uncertainty, and optimization for talent, just as it does for financial investments.

Strategic workforce planning systems have an untapped capacity to optimize talent capability when an organization is faced with future risk. This chapter shows how scenario planning and risk-optimization tools from finance can create that capacity. Chapter 1 showed how the engineering concept of return on improved performance (ROIP) can help you identify where the quality of your human capital makes the greatest difference, considering *one* future strategic situation. This chapter extends that idea, connecting HR systems to tools that can consider several future strategic situations at once.

Find Risk Before It Finds You

Risk is often seen as a four-letter word, but it is a good idea to embrace it, understand it, and use it to achieve important goals. The financial turmoil of 2008 revealed that most organizations' strategies needed to consider much broader future possibilities. Michael Jackson, the CEO of AutoNation, arrived in 2001 when the auto industry was selling 17 million units annually. Yet at his very first management meeting he announced his intention to find a business model that would let AutoNation survive even if the industry sold only 10 million units. He challenged his team to consider a scenario that was radically different from anything they had experienced, and to consider what would be the most significant factors that would cause it, and how to address it. By 2008, of course, the wisdom of this approach was apparent.

> Everybody looked at me like I had six heads," he recalls. "Eventually, we came to the conclusion that, among other things, it would take a credit crisis to get volumes that low, because in our business, nothing moves without credit. So we got out of the finance and leasing business," says Jackson. "Without the limitation on risk we put in place, we would be in deep, serious trouble at the moment.[1]

Jackson used classic logic for evaluating risk and return:

1. Describe alternative future scenarios ("we sell only 10 million cars").

2. Examine the causes and estimate the probabilities of those scenarios ("credit crunch").

3. Determine the value of the current investments under all scenarios ("AutoNation's finance and leasing business is a cash cow with cheap credit, but a devastating loss in a credit crunch").

4. Choose investments that maximize the expected return considering all the scenarios ("divesting finance and leasing has the higher expected value, considering the likelihood of tighter credit").

The key to such scenario planning is not that it predicts the future perfectly, nor that the probabilities of scenarios are known. Jackson did not *know* that the financial crisis would occur, but he identified a way for AutoNation to hedge against the possibility.

Scenarios are not expected to predict the future perfectly, but to motivate creative thinking.[2] The value of scenarios is that they encourage you to think broadly about the greatest potential threats and opportunities and consider what would have to change, and how to take action or to hedge against threats and capitalize on opportunities. These are the strategic pivot points. For Auto-Nation, future success would look very different in a cheap credit scenario versus a credit crisis, and whether AutoNation owned the financing and leasing business was the pivotal factor.

Strategic workforce planning systems are very good at identifying talent implications *after* a future scenario has been chosen. For example, at AutoNation, once the divestiture decision was made, the talent implications could be identified and HR programs put in place to deal with them. As with designing an investment strategy for other resources, however, strategic workforce planning can consider alternative scenarios—*before* the decision is made—to identify the pivotal workforce and organization design elements that would change the most in various future situations.

For AutoNation, certain talent and organization elements varied a lot depending on whether there was plentiful cheap credit versus a credit shortage. In a scenario of limited credit, Auto-Nation's customer representatives and online designers would need to perform better in helping buyers find auto dealers or car sellers willing to extend credit, or helping buyers analyze their own finances to afford their car purchase; moreover, AutoNation leaders might need to lobby governments for tax breaks and financial incentives, such as the Cash for Clunkers program of 2009. In contrast, a scenario of abundant credit would mean that customer representatives and online designers would need skills in structuring credit arrangements and extolling the advantages of Auto-Nation's credit and leasing business, and AutoNation leaders would need skills in managing credit and leasing operations.

AutoNation leaders could therefore use strategic workforce planning to generate a talent strategy for each scenario, identifying the workforce and organization pivot points that would change a lot, and those that wouldn't, under the various future conditions.

Dealing with Talent Risk

Talent is costly, and the time horizon to build skills, competencies, learning, leadership, alignment, and other talent outcomes is usually longer than the time horizon over which we can make good predictions. Consider how long it takes to acquire and develop skilled technical professionals, leaders, plant managers, or even the supervisors of customer-facing retail or call center associates. Now consider how far in the future your strategy projects. Usually, the reach of your strategy is much shorter than the time it takes to build the talent.

An executive in a global technology services firm put it this way:

Increasingly, we must stay more fluid in our development recommendations to our employees. For example, our businesses might see more projects that need systems architects with a deep understanding of local selling systems. We'll encourage our systems architects and selling experts to join multi-year development programs to get qualified for these future roles. Our systems architects will start learning more about personal selling, and our salespeople will start developing systems expertise. However, in our business, things can change in a year, if new technology develops or our client priorities change. After a year, personal selling may become less important, with the rise of viral marketing through web-based user-generated content. Our employees are one year into a three-year program, based on our prediction of a growing market for systems architects with personal local selling expertise. Now, things have changed, and they need to switch gears and prepare for a viral marketing future.[3]

No matter how sophisticated your workforce planning and development systems are, the past is not a perfect predictor of the future ("what got you here may not get you there"). Workforce and organizational capabilities develop over long time horizons, so talent capability may face a future that is very different from the one predicted when the investments were made. Faced with an uncertain future, organizations often respond with talent strategies that extrapolate from the past, prepare for the most likely future, stick to generic capabilities that apply to virtually any future, or build agile talent that will flex to fit whatever future presents itself. Let's look at each of these approaches.

Keep Doing What Worked Before

Many organizations simply assume that the future will resemble the past and continue to make talent investments that were successful before. This is often the lowest-cost strategy. Existing HR systems are in place, things are working well, and the costs and disruption of changing are obvious. This is particularly tempting when things are going well (like AutoNation in 2001).

Strategic workforce planning always recognizes that things may change, so HR leaders can often see the danger of staying with what has worked. However, HR stakeholders, lacking a specific way to consider the talent implications of alternative futures, may mistakenly extrapolate from the past, because for them, avoiding costs and disruptions is the most tangible goal.

Prepare for the Most Probable Future

When strategic workforce planning considers a future different from the past, it often chooses only one.[4] With that scenario in hand, the system can project likely talent supply, talent demand, talent gaps, and the investments to reduce them.

Figure 2-1 shows a typical workforce planning model used by several organizations. It is sophisticated in its attention to business strategy connections and scenario planning and to ongoing review to detect and respond to changes.

Such systems often produce one particular workforce strategy rather than several strategies reflecting multiple future scenarios.

FIGURE 2-1

A typical workforce planning model

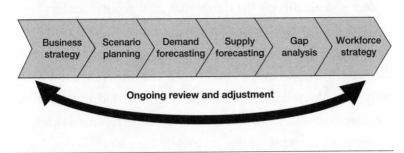

Business strategy › Scenario planning › Demand forecasting › Supply forecasting › Gap analysis › Workforce strategy

Ongoing review and adjustment

Fitting workforce and talent strategies to the most likely future scenario is a good approach if the scenario you choose is highly likely. However, what if several future scenarios are highly probable? Many workforce planning systems can adjust as conditions change, but it implies that you'll know more later, and that may not be true.

Go Generic to Fit Multiple Futures

When you're faced with several highly likely alternative future conditions, perhaps the best strategy is to invest in talent so that it will fit a wide variety of future possibilities. This is like holding a portfolio of cash or cash-equivalent investments, knowing that they will hold their value in all future economic conditions. Adopting competency systems based on generic traits and attributes, or hiring based on general intelligence, fits this approach. Many leadership competency systems are built on attributes such as vision, communication, emotional intelligence, decisiveness, and so on.

Authors in the field of talent management and leadership have lamented the fact that the competency systems of various organizations look much like those of their competitors, reducing the chance for an organization to be strategically unique. This happens when you define competencies by examining diverse sets of leaders and identifying the things that all successful leaders have in common. It's like looking for the attributes of good swimmers by studying all swimmers, whether they're doing the breaststroke, the butterfly stroke, or the crawl stroke.[5] Elements such as upper-body strength, cardiovascular fitness, and poise under pressure are certainly common to all successful swimmers. Yet in a swimming competition, the attribute that determines the winner is often determined by who is better at the specific stroke that fits that race.

Generic competencies and other talent attributes serve an important purpose; they have value in a wide array of situations. HR leaders and their stakeholders may find it attractive to invest in systems that build generic talent attributes, figuring that by doing so they ensure that the organization's talent will have some value under any future conditions. The generic strategy is less risky in that sense, but it misses the potentially high payoff that would come from having talent specifically suited to the future that does occur.

Often, HR stakeholders choose generic without considering what they might be missing. It is a mistake to invest generically if one future is so likely that it is the better bet, or if you could diversify the risk in better ways. Financial investment frameworks explicitly anticipate and help leaders articulate such choices and then choose with awareness of the trade-offs.

Match Uncertainty with Agility

A third approach for developing a strategy to deal with an uncertain future is to be flexible enough to handle future contingencies. Recall in figure 2-1 that the company's planning system included ongoing review and adjustment precisely to be more agile. This is the most frequent approach that HR and business leaders describe when I ask them what they are doing to build talent for a more uncertain future. They say, "We can't predict the future, so we are building HR programs to increase adaptability and agility among all of our employees, and throughout our culture and systems, so that they can change with future conditions."

Ron Parker, executive vice president of human resources at Pepsi, puts it this way: "You cannot stay in a steady state in a competitive global environment. That which is not broken today should be broken tomorrow. We look at the entire value chain and are constantly asking ourselves what needs to change. Leaders need to be asking themselves the same questions: How and what do I need to change to keep up with the future and to be of value to this organization?"[6]

A *BusinessWeek* article suggests that the answer is to place agile learners throughout the organization: "Agile learners . . . thrive in new and difficult situations. They are clear thinkers who know themselves well and like to experiment. They also like to learn and can quickly apply new knowledge. Most importantly— and not surprisingly—agile learners deliver results, even in new situations . . . But no matter how learning agile you are, you're not going to make all the right calls yourself, whether you're in charge of 10 people or 50,000. So it's equally important to develop agile learners at all levels of your organization."[7]

Agility is important, but having agile learners everywhere is expensive. The principles of return on improved performance (ROIP) discussed in chapter 1 suggest that agility is more pivotal in some places than in others. Making a similar point in operations management, one management science book says that simply assuming that flexible manufacturing processes will address uncertainty about the future is "tantamount to a strategic cop-out."[8] Too much agility can actually cause problems. Is it really necessary for most organizations to have the most agile accountants? Also, just how far can leaders and employees stretch in response to changes in strategy, markets, or conditions?

Recall the Boeing example in chapter 1. Engineers or contract managers who are capable of facilitating cooperation across the supply chain may be very different from those who are good at traditional technical engineering or contract auditing. Can one type transform into the other type simply by being agile learners? Perhaps, but a strategic workforce planning system should offer tools to specifically consider this question, and not simply add more agility to the plan.

Relying on agile learning is best if the future will become clearer later and you'll have time to adjust to it when it is clearer. Agility is also better when a particular future isn't so likely that you should simply bet on that one. If HR systems can help articulate these choices, HR stakeholders are less likely to make well-meaning investments in agility when it isn't the strategy most likely to succeed.

Talent Diversification

Can you bet on more than one future at the same time? Can you hedge your bets by preparing for all of them? AutoNation could have hedged its bets by preparing its talent for a future of abundant credit as well as a future with a credit shortage. The company could have developed leaders, salespeople, and online designers having the competencies for both future scenarios. Or the company could have developed a workforce having a mixture of talent—some suited for an easy-credit future, and others for a credit-constrained future.

One or the other group would be underutilized, depending on which future AutoNation eventually faced, but it may be more effective to carry both types of talent in the portfolio rather than stay with the past, build for a new future, or try to increase agility—in other words, diversify, a topic we turn to next.

When Workforce Diversification Makes Sense

In financial analysis, *diversification* means holding multiple assets that behave differently under various future market conditions. The three strategies just discussed are types of diversification. Betting on the past or the most probable future is a decision to limit diversification to one asset class in hopes of a big payoff if you are right. Building generically is a decision to diversify to assets that produce an equal and payoff in many possible futures. Relying on agility is a decision to bet on one future at a time but to use investments that can be quickly liquidated and replaced. However, a fourth approach is actually to hold multiple asset classes that effectively optimize the risk of multiple futures.

Diversification combines investments to produce combinations that deal with multiple future possibilities to optimize risk and return.[9] How can strategic workforce planning become more like portfolio diversification?

Ontario Hydro: Making the
Right Bet on a Leadership Team

The failure of a large nuclear reactor run by Ontario Power Generation (OPG) in Canada was associated with the board's choice in hiring a leadership team. Should the board hire a team that was adept at accomplishing an IPO and privatization (a goal that had been set by the Ontario government), or a team that was adept at managing a nuclear energy company? The board chose the former, with the result that serious technical problems—caused by the leadership's lack of experience in the field—led to the shutdown of several reactors:

> The government was focused on recruiting a CEO who could launch a new public company, but ignored the fact that he lacked experience with the nuclear problems he also confronted . . . Most of the utility's recent directors were recruited in the 1990s to help privatize OPG, with several bringing solid financing experience to the IPO, which never occurred. None had nuclear expertise.[10]

The decision to build a leadership team with the right mix—in this case, of IPO and plant operational capability—is the same idea as building a portfolio containing diversified securities. If the Ontario Hydro IPO of OPG had happened as planned, the failure never would have occurred because the bet on a leadership team adept at IPOs would have been right. The question of strategic workforce planning faced by the power company board was how to make the best decision before knowing what would happen. A portfolio manager would say that the right decision might have been for the government and board members to invest in both IPO and nuclear operations capability in the leadership team, using diversification to offset the risk of both future scenarios, knowing that some of the leadership team skills would not fit perfectly.

The Ontario Hydro case illustrates three conditions that make portfolio diversification tools crucial for strategic workforce planning. First, the IPO and the operational challenges required differing leadership team capabilities. Ontario Hydro's board did not have the luxury of hiring people whose capabilities were well suited to both challenges. Second, the alternative future scenarios were well defined. The IPO scenario and the nuclear operations scenario both had specific leadership implications.

Third, more than one future scenario had a high probability. The board could be reasonably sure that either the IPO or the nuclear operations scenario would occur, and each of them had a high enough probability to be relevant. When these conditions exist, betting on only one scenario may be more risky than betting on several, and pursuing a generic talent approach may miss significant opportunities. Betting on both may be more optimal.

Williams-Sonoma: Making the Right Bet on Store Managers

Now consider a very different example: the frontline talent in a multiple-location retail organization. It often takes a very different type of store manager to handle a large store than a small store. John Bronson, former head of HR for Williams-Sonoma, explains:

> As I worked on the performance assessment for store managers, I realized that a 3,0000-square-foot store required a very different type of store manager than a 6,000-square-foot store. There is a strong "promote-from-within" culture at Williams-Sonoma which has served it well over the years. The best Sales Associates were identified for advancement, and they were given assignments beyond sales that would prepare them to become Store General Managers (Store GMs). At the DNA level, the best Sales Associates were very focused on providing great customer service. And the great ones were also highly self-motivated. If you put these two traits together, a shorthand description would be "Type-A Pleasers." This is a highly enviable combination in sales associates in any business, but not for a General Manager. What I came to recognize was that with these traits alone, Store

GMs survived in some situations, and failed in others. It was the issue of scale of the store. Store GMs who were "Type-A-Pleasers" could survive in the smaller store format purely through "heroic intervention," stepping in and rolling up their sleeves when their sales associates weren't getting the job done themselves. Delegation was a nice but not essential skill in small stores. However, in a larger store it was just the opposite. A Store GM simply could not be everywhere at once in a larger store. If he or she tried to do the work themselves, they would fail. To succeed in the large store format required a third trait—delegations skills; Store GMs had to be able to drive results through others. Poor performers had to be addressed and either improved or terminated. Consistent with the promote-from-within policy, it was typical to promote Store GMs who had been successful in small stores to the larger stores, which were often twice as large as the store from which they were promoted. We realized that the small-store manager and large-store manager jobs were actually two very different jobs, and the person who would excel in one would not necessarily excel in the other. The effect of promoting small-store GMs from what was essentially a high-level individual contributor into a job that required delegation and performance management was extremely costly. Not only did we end up with under performance in the larger stores, but we ended up losing Store GMs who never should have been promoted to the larger store format.[11]

Like many retailers, Williams-Sonoma had a portfolio diversification problem. In large stores the ROIP on delegation was far higher than the ROIP on doing the work, and it was just the opposite in small stores. The company needed the right future mix of small- and large-store managers, but it had to start building those capabilities long before it could be certain how many of each type of store it would have. Betting wrong would be costly.

China Business Expansion: Betting on Global Leadership

Organizations throughout the world face choices about the types of leaders to develop in the face of uncertain futures regarding global development. A McKinsey & Company report on the talent implications of growth in China provides a good example of the situation facing most global organizations:

> The functional skills and leadership abilities required in China will probably differ from those called for in developed markets. Managers in China might, for example, need to know more about simplifying or tailoring products, finding low-capital solutions, and managing alliances and government relations. A higher level of comfort with ambiguity or greater cultural openness may be necessary as well. Companies in China must therefore be prepared to recognize and address the difference between their talent needs in that country and in the rest of the world.[12]

Table 2-1 shows how each of the talent situations I've described here can be retooled using portfolio diversification logic. Classic portfolio logic says that financial investments are choices about holding combinations of security assets, facing uncertain future economic conditions. Ontario Hydro faced a choice of having IPO or nuclear operations capabilities in its OPG leadership team, amid uncertainty about whether the IPO would happen. Williams-Sonoma faced choices about holding combinations of store managers, amid future uncertainty about how many big versus small stores it would operate. Organizations working in China

TABLE 2-1

How talent decisions look like financial diversification decisions

Situation	Financial portfolio holdings	Ontario Hydro leadership team	Williams-Sonoma store managers	Global organization leadership
Uncertain future scenarios	Economic conditions	IPO or nuclear plan operation	High or low percentage of large stores	Chinese markets grow quickly, moderately, or slowly
Choices	What mix of assets should I hold?	What mix of IPO and operational capabilities should I hire in the leadership team?	What mix of competencies should I hire or develop among store managers?	What mix of China-ready future leaders should I hire or develop?

face choices about hiring or developing unknown numbers of China-ready leaders, amid uncertainty about how much business they will do in China.

Each case shows the three conditions that make risk optimization vital. The possible future challenges require different talent capabilities and have well-defined talent implications, and several of the scenarios are likely enough to be relevant.

Strategic Portfolio Analysis for Developing Economies

The China situation described in the *McKinsey Quarterly* article is of widespread concern, but the challenge doesn't apply only to China. It is part of a much larger global talent strategy dilemma. The talent and leadership style needed in developing countries is often very different from what is needed in developed countries, and the eventual size of developing country markets versus developed country markets is uncertain. This dilemma is useful for illustrating the power of using portfolio tools to retool strategic workforce planning under uncertainty.

An HR executive at a global high-tech company put it well:

> We are creating brand-building talent that will be very suited to a world in which we have about 70% of our business in developed countries and about 30% in emerging countries. If emerging-country business growth is below 30%, our brand-building talent strategy will fit. However, if emerging markets grow much faster than we expect, our three-year talent investment won't fit as well. If I knew for sure we'd see emerging-country revenues of 50% or more in the next five years, I [would] change how we invest in brand-building talent development today. We're investing for the future that is most likely, but the alternative is not impossible.[13]

Of course, some standard competencies will always be useful in both types of markets, but developing markets require greater capability to lead across cultures, greater expertise in microfinance, products that fit a certain low price point, different expertise styles to manage less mature legal, information, or distribution infrastructures, and a higher tolerance for risk.

Imagine doing the ROIP analysis of chapter 1 for key positions, considering the value of performance first in developed markets and then in developing markets. The ROIP curves for several roles and work performance elements would undoubtedly vary greatly between the two scenarios. Other roles or work performance elements would look similar, requiring no choices. Where there are differences, though, leaders must decide whether to build the capabilities that fit developing markets, the capabilities that fit developed markets, or some combination.

Stakeholders at the high-tech company just quoted were admonishing HR to be agile, to wait until the future was more certain, and then to quickly create the necessary talent needed for the markets that emerged. These company leaders did not want to bear the long-term cost of developing brand-building talent when such talent might not fit the future. These stakeholders were like day traders in the stock market, wanting to spend resources to stay flexible and constantly vigilant. Yet my HR colleague knew that once the developing economies boomed and competition for talent became intense, it would be expensive and difficult to attract and retain developing country brand managers on short notice. It would be much easier and less costly to build brand managers having the needed expertise over several years' time.

Other stakeholders said, "Let's just keep doing what we're doing and take our chances, because we already have those systems in place." They were like "buy and hold" investors, minimizing transaction costs and preferring to stay for the long term after a decision was made. Like buy and hold, this talent portfolio approach would avoid the costs of changing talent strategies and would require less vigilance compared with the agility strategy, but it risked missing opportunities if the past didn't fit the future.

A third group of stakeholders, particularly those working in developing countries, passionately argued that HR should immediately start developing brand-building talent for developing economies, describing in great detail the missed opportunities they feared if they didn't have that talent available when hyper-growth occurred. This group was similar to investors who want to liquidate their current holdings and move fully into a portfolio suited to developing economies. This strategy would allow the organization to get in early while talent costs were lower, but it would incur costs to make the change, it would take time to develop the talent, and it risked having the new approach not fit the future if markets didn't grow as rapidly as expected.

How should HR and its stakeholders determine the best strategy? Ideally, collaboration is best. HR planners need to collaborate with stakeholders who have deep knowledge about emerging
economies. HR needs to avoid making the decision alone, and instead help country-savvy business leaders be more adept and more
accountable for the bet to be placed on brand-building talent. The
tools of portfolio diversification offer a way to create objective,
logical, and productive discussions, using a language that leaders
are already familiar with, and that has been used for years to help
solve similar dilemmas when it comes to financial investments.

Optimizing Risk and Return for
Global Brand-Building Talent

Table 2-2 recasts the global brand-building talent dilemma as a
portfolio diversification decision. There are three future scenarios,
describing high ($60 billion), moderate ($30 billion), and low
($20 billion) projected revenues in the developing economy mar-
ket, with probabilities of 30 percent, 50 percent, and 20 percent,

TABLE 2-2

**Portfolio diversification analysis for global brand-building
talent strategies**

Strategic scenario (3-year market in developing countries)	Probability of strategic scenario	Returns from 100% developed economy talent strategy	Returns from 100% developing economy talent strategy	Returns from 100% generic talent strategy	Returns from 65% developed and 35% developing combination
$60 billion	30%	20 points[a]	130 points	40 points	59 points
$30 billion	50%	50 points	70 points	40 points	57 points
$20 billion	20%	100 points	–20 points	40 points	58 points
Expected return		51 points	70 points	40 points	58 points

a. Satisfaction points. See text.

respectively. The organization had to decide whether to (1) invest in talent strategies to create brand-building talent for developing economies, developed economies, or a combination, or to (2) go with generic brand-building capabilities, or to (3) wait and try to move with agility when the future was known.

Estimating the Risk and Return of Each Talent Strategy

The value of talent strategies under varying future scenarios cannot be calculated as precisely as the return on investment in a financial instrument or physical plant. The logic of return on investment is clear, including projected costs, projected effects on organizational objectives, and a discount factor to reflect how benefits and costs would be incurred over time. As HR systems mature, it will be easier to estimate talent strategy returns. But even imperfect numbers that reflect stakeholders' own best estimates can tap the power of diversification tools.

For this example, suppose we assign 100 *satisfaction points* to the scenario that will best fit our current strategy of investing in developed economy brand-building talent. That is the future in which we make $20 billion in developing economy revenue, combined with a strategy of a 100 percent investment in brand-building talent for developed economies. We bet right if developing economy revenues turn out to be low and we did not invest in developing economy brand-building talent.

Then we could ask stakeholders to consider the factors that affect the returns on talent investments, including the costs and the regret and satisfaction they would feel if talent is mismatched or well-matched to the eventual situation. Table 2-2 shows hypothetical points assigned to each of the two strategies under each future condition. For the strategy of 100 percent developed economy talent, the points fall from 100 to 50 to 20 as the revenues from developing economies increase. For the strategy of 100% developing economy talent, the satisfaction points are 130 if we bet right and developing economies are huge, 70 if they grow moderately, and −20 if they are only $20 billion. The reason for the wider range is that investing to build developing economy talent means making expensive changes to current practices, so if we bet wrong we are even less happy than if we stay with our current strategy.

We can calculate the average or "expected" satisfaction-point score for each strategy by multiplying the satisfaction points by the probability of the future scenario. For the 100% developed economy talent strategy, the expected value is 51 points. For the 100% developing economy strategy, the expected value is 70 points. It is higher even though we will have a −20 satisfaction level if we bet wrong, because the payoff is so high if we bet right.

The risk in these talent strategies is now clearer. The wider the swing in satisfaction across future scenarios, the more uncertainty and the more regret we will experience if we bet wrong. The strategy of investing 100% in developing economy talent has a wider range of possible outcomes, but the payoff is much higher returns if we are right.

Again, it is important not to get fixated on whether the satisfaction points (or any other estimate of returns on talent investments) are perfectly accurate. Even with these hypothetical satisfaction points, we can see patterns, such as the wider variation for the developing economy talent strategy and the relative spread in satisfaction across scenarios for each strategy. If stakeholders estimate a narrow spread for one strategy versus the other, that would tell us that stakeholders see one strategy as playing it safe, and the other as a big gamble. If we see numbers that are very similar for both strategies, that would suggest stakeholders will be indifferent to the choice, so we could decide based only on costs. The point is not to generate precise numbers but to prompt productive and logical conversations about future possibilities.

Retooling Talent Strategy Discussions:
Stay, Bet, or Go Generic

Faced with decisions like the brand-building example, leaders may be tempted to pursue talent strategy options without careful consideration and discussion. Table 2-2 helps us see that the "stay with the past" strategy of building developed economy brand-building competencies is indeed less risky than betting on developing economy talent, but it comes at a significant reduction in satisfaction for two of the scenarios. The "bet on the future" strategy of building developing economy talent carries risk, but only if revenues from developing economies turn out to be at their lowest levels. The portfolio framework invites a specific conversation about risks and returns.

A "go generic" strategy in this case would create talent development approaches that build generic brand-building capabilities that apply in developed as well as developing economies, but it does not invest in specific capabilities for either one. Stakeholders might estimate that the generic strategy would get 40 satisfaction points under any future conditions, as table 2-2 shows. That's a little more value than the developed country strategy when it's wrong (20 points) but not as much as the developed country strategy with moderate growth (50 points). It's a risk-free decision that is most wrong if developing markets do very well.

Portfolio Diversification for Talent:
Playing Multiple Futures

It might seem illogical to invest in both strategies, knowing that only one of them will be needed. Yet, as with financial assets, investing in both can actually be a very good decision, especially when choices are difficult because the returns move in opposite directions. Because it may cost more to pursue two talent strategies at once, this option is often dismissed without analysis even though it is a popular strategy for investing in other resources. Reframing strategic workforce planning more like a financial investment helps leaders see the whole picture.

The sixth column in table 2-2 shows the opportunity. What would happen if the organization invested 65 percent in developed economy and 35 percent in developing economy brand-building talent capability? In each future scenario, the organization's total return would be a mix of 35 percent of the return from the developing economy talent and 65 percent of the return from the developed economy talent. The table shows that the returns in every scenario are similar, ranging from 57 to 59. This "35-65" diversified talent strategy produces a higher expected return (58 satisfaction points) than staying with a 100 percent developed economy strategy or choosing the generic strategy (40 points), and yet the diversified strategy carries very low risk. That's the power of diversification, and it explains why pursuing a mix of talent strategies may be more optimum than pursuing a generic strategy or choosing between them.

What would it mean to pursue a 35-65 combination of brand-building talent? It might mean hiring 35 percent of future brand-building talent in developing economies and 65 percent in developed economies. It might mean that 35 percent of brand-building training programs would focus on developing economy skills and 65 percent on developed economy skills. Similar approaches could be created for rewards, careers, and performance management. This is not the same as simply pursuing brand-building talent for each region, with the mix of developing economy and developed economy talent suited to each region's needs. The prudent choice may be to overstaff in developing regions to create a talent surplus that will satisfy future needs.

Starbucks, for example, developed scenarios using matrices built on various combinations of two dimensions that define the future. Let's consider a hypothetical use of such a matrix. Suppose the company considers the four futures defined by two dimensions: (1) insourcing versus outsourcing distribution; combined with (2) lean manufacturing increasing productivity or not. Then in each quadrant the Starbucks planners expanded the workforce implications, asking questions such as, "How will these changes affect the employment brand, our organization climate, the work environment, and internal movement or attrition patterns?" "How will it change which talent segments will exist in our future workforce?" "How might our rewards strategy have to change?"[14] A diversified talent strategy seeks the same alignment of HR practices, but now they are aligned with an optimum strategic talent *combination*.[15]

Mayank Jain, director of human resources, Human Capital Planning at Ameriprise Financial, a global financial services company, noted the similarity between the idea of a portfolio of asset classes and its potential application in talent planning decisions concerning the portfolio of asset managers in financial services companies. In their wealth management business, companies like Ameriprise compete to manage large institutional portfolios, such as pension funds. The asset managers who are experts in different types of assets are generally not fungible but instead are highly specialized. So such companies must in essence create the right portfolio of asset managers to fit the likely future asset-class management challenges where they want to compete. Many wealth management businesses portray themselves to their clients in a certain light in terms of risk-return philosophy, such as Moderately Aggressive, Aggressive, Conservative, and so on. This categorization has specific implications about the sorts of asset classes and combinations that the company will need to manage.

Therefore, companies like Ameriprise Financial can optimize their asset manager talent combinations based on future scenarios that reflect potential economic conditions, client desires, evolving financial instruments, and cross-asset synergies. As Jain puts it, "it is not just that we need to say that our asset managers individually are leaders among their peers. It is common for clients to consider a team of asset managers, and the range of investment strategies, horizons, and markets we're prepared to compete in. Our decisions about the combination of asset managers we will need should be similar to our strategic decisions regarding which asset classes and combinations our clients will require. This enables us to best meet client needs, and optimize against the uncertainties about what requirements will eventually arise."[16]

These examples can be extended to take into account other risk management tools, such as insurance, options, and optimizing talent investments against the volatility of the industry or region in which they will be deployed. Game theory, a classic academic tool for evaluating uncertain situations that depend on sequential decisions by competitors, is re-emerging as a way to balance risks and opportunities against multiple futures.[17] Talent strategy, like strategies for managing money, customers, and technology, can exploit decades of learning in other business disciplines that has long been used to optimize, not merely mitigate, risk. HR's stakeholders are accustomed to thinking this way about other resources, so why not think this way about talent?

How HR Leaders Can Use Portfolio Optimization to Retool Strategic Workforce Planning

As an HR leader, you are already using strategic workforce planning systems to plan for a single future, so you can develop the same forecasting and gap analysis to plan for several future scenarios and then assess them using the probabilities that strategic planners assign to those scenarios. Of course, multiple-scenario planning is time-consuming, so it should be focused on those situations wherein strategic leaders agree that there are multiple futures with high probability that may present greatly differing talent implications. Simply asking these questions helps you find areas where betting on one scenario may be risky, and this kind of discovery in itself can prevent mistakes.

To focus portfolio tools where they are likely to produce their greatest insight, ask questions like these:

- Which three to five scenarios are probable and imply the greatest differences in our organization or business-unit strategy?

- What are the strategic issues that will make the greatest differences across the scenarios? How will those issues differ with each scenario?

- Which talent and organizational areas will differ most across those pivotal strategic elements?

- What are the most significant differences in our human resource strategies and practices across those talent and organization differences?

You can embrace imperfect and qualitative data. Portfolio logic frames talent decisions as investments, and leaders are accustomed to imperfect data in other investment areas. Table 2-2, presented earlier, uses satisfaction points as a way to get stakeholders to articulate relative returns. Precise numbers may not yield the greatest insight. Melissa Cummings, who leads Aetna's strategic workforce program, put it this way: "Analytics has thrown a veil over what passes for workforce planning . . . Data is about what happened in the past. Forecasting is a static vision of the future. We take data and forecasts and build on them with 'what ifs' to create a richer vision. That's the qualitative piece that the enterprise needs."[18]

You can facilitate a richer strategy discussion among your peers in corporate strategy, finance, and other key functions. Aetna's strategic planning group engages teams of fifteen to twenty business leaders to consider environmental and company data and then construct scenario matrices. One axis reflects factors that are out of the company's control, such as the economy, and the second axis shows factors within its control, such as how the company positions itself geographically. The participants look at alternative scenarios and outcomes for the four quadrants and then generate reports. "We talk about the themes in each quadrant and that helps us look at possible future needs," Cummings says. "Once you get there, it's easier to see the goals and build an action plan." HR may well become the catalyst for deeper scenario planning through its desire to develop detailed scenarios that clearly connect to various talent implications.

How Business Leaders Can Use Portfolio Optimization to Retool Strategic Workforce Planning

As a leader outside HR, you need to embrace risk when it comes to the organization's talent. You must become more adept and accountable for long-term talent bets that have uncertain payoffs, just as you do for other resources. Choosing a generic talent strategy because it's popular with other companies, or staying with past strategies to save money, should not be an acceptable strategy for managing talent any more than it would be for managing other resources.

As an HR stakeholder, you must accept the fact that a healthy level of risk means that not all talent decisions will be the right bet, just as decisions about other resources can turn out wrong.

Stakeholders have a right to use tools that help them consider alternatives logically and to be given credit for decisions that make sense, even if they mean betting on two different futures.

You should ask, "What if . . .?" as much as, "What does HR recommend?" Elegant talent forecasts and gap analysis focused on single scenarios are enticing, but a risk profile having less accuracy and greater comprehensiveness may be more valuable than overly precise plans that fail to account for risk. Your most important role as a partner with HR may be to think creatively about potential disruptions, threats, and opportunities, and not press HR for its plan of action too early.

You should define your talent dilemmas using the logic you use for other investment decisions. What future scenarios imply the greatest potential differences in your business unit or organization? What are the probabilities of those scenarios? Have you communicated those to your HR planners? What kind of talent takes a long time to develop, and where should you be taking calculated risks to prepare for the future? Where can you pursue a generic strategy until the future becomes clear, and where do you need to make a bet? If you ask your HR leaders to "stay agile" until the future is clearer, are you willing to bear the cost of realigning talent on short notice? How might you combine talent investments to hedge against excessive risk, and are you prepared to carry several different categories of talent assets to do that?

Strategic workforce planning can tap great value as a tool for considering multiple futures and designing the optimum talent mix to meet them. The raw materials for talent strategies are in place, because HR systems already make elegant forecasts based on single scenarios. The next step is to do that for multiple scenarios, to become adept at knowing when such deep analysis is most needed, and to use the results to focus on talent diversification beyond talent planning.

Opportunities to Improve HR

- Facilitate a better connection between strategic workforce planning and strategic scenarios.

- Optimize workforce capabilities for future uncertainty through diversification.

- Recast talent management investments as hedges against future risk.

- Measure and report workforce data such as competencies, potential, skills, and capabilities like "asset classes" in financial strategy.

Opportunities to Improve HR's Connection with Stakeholders

- Connect strategic planning scenarios more directly with workforce and talent decisions.

- Make stakeholders accountable and adept at making workforce investments under uncertainty, just as with financial investments.

- Make stakeholders more accountable and adept at preparing talent capability for multiple future scenarios simultaneously.

3

Using Consumer Research to Retool Talent Supply Strategies

From Let's Make an iDeal to Optimized

Talent Segmentation

This chapter addresses the supply side of strategic workforce planning to show how HR leaders and stakeholders can transform strategic workforce supply planning from forecasting future supply to influencing it. Organizations are awash in information about the external environment, employment patterns, demographics, and generational differences as well as growing data about the internal labor market, including employee engagement, performance levels, and movement patterns. All of this information has the potential to help companies manage and even optimize the supply of talent, if HR leaders exploit the power of marketing tools that do this for consumers and customer segments. How can companies use that information to manage their supply of employees?

Organizations influence talent supply patterns through the *employment deal* they offer various talent segments: specific individuals, groups, roles, generations, and so on. Employee behaviors include joining, staying, moving, and leaving an organization's employ. Employment features range from the tangible to the intangible and include pay, benefits, training, culture, leadership quality, and organization mission, as well as the informal recognition, feedback, and development opportunities that hinge on the daily decisions of managers and leaders.

HR leaders and stakeholders can take a variety of approaches to designing the employment deal, including matching what top organizations do, offering employees and applicants what they say they want, fixing problems identified by departing employees, or responding to the differing desires of generations and cultures. Often, though, HR stakeholders simply follow standard rules, telling employees, "I'd love to help you, but HR won't let me." Or they hear about attractive-sounding innovations at a company voted "best to work for" and ask HR to offer the same perks to their employees. For HR stakeholders, the considerations are often local, because they know their people well and know which offerings would attract, retain, and motivate them. Or at the other extreme, leaders and managers can vividly see the disruption caused by making "special deals," so they avoid them altogether.

Organizations face the same dilemmas when local leaders wish to change branding or product features to enhance sales in their markets, but there are larger considerations about global brands, cross-regional relationships, and price-cost trade-offs that may not be visible to local managers. In the case of products, marketing tools provide a way to convey the more comprehensive set of considerations, making leaders more adept and accountable for such decisions.

When HR stakeholders customize or standardize where it's unwise, the costs are often borne and seen by the HR organization, so stakeholders can be forgiven for not considering costs when they ask for new perks or refuse to consider deviating from the standard rules. In the same way, HR also has insights, often not visible to stakeholders, about the patterns of workforce and applicant preferences that can help stakeholders better understand and explain why some groups should and do receive different treatment. Putting the two perspectives together often reveals powerful ways to influence the supply and quality of talent, but that requires tools that connect preferences, responses, and segmentation to optimize the impact of employment offerings.

Optimizing offerings rests on three questions:

- What are the pivotal talent segments?

- What response do we need from those talent segments?

- What features of the employment deal create the best response at the lowest cost?

In marketing and consumer research, these three questions are used to optimize the deal that matches product and service features to the preferences of customer segments; the goal is to choose features that maximize lifetime profitability of a product or service by balancing their costs against customer purchases, loyalty, and other behaviors (buying more, paying more, recommending to others, etc.). In the same way, these marketing tools offer HR and its stakeholders a way to connect the costs and the impact of investments in employment offerings that influence the strategic talent supply.

Should You Mass-Customize
Your Employment Deal?

Google is famous for its uniquely vast array of employee benefits.

> One Google worker, Gopi Kallayil, senior product market-
> ing manager, says he eats the gourmet food for "breakfast,
> lunch and dinner" on the company's dime. He hasn't gotten
> around to working with the free personal trainer or using the
> swimming pool or spa, and he doesn't need to ride Google
> shuttle bus, but he works out at the Google fitness center,
> takes advantage of the speaker series, and visits the in-house
> doctor, nutritionist, dry cleaner, and massage service, all at
> no charge.[1]

Google's employees work long hours, are extremely loyal, and
have low turnover. Would your organization leaders assume that
the cure for insufficient numbers or poorly performing knowledge
workers is to duplicate Google's approach? Or would some of
those leaders dismiss Google's approach as the folly of an organization with more money than sense, and demand quantitative evidence that connects such investments to tangible employee and
business outcomes?

Google illustrates one dilemma for organization leaders: increasingly, the employment deal is being expanded with creative new
features that go well beyond the traditional wages, hours, and working conditions. How should firms combine the infinite variety of
possibilities?

This question is at least as old as the idea of *cafeteria benefits*,
in which employees are given choices among insurance types and
features, often using pretax dollars to pay for insurance or other
benefits. The idea is that employees are the best judges of what
most motivates and retains them, and they will better appreciate

the value of the benefits they choose. Employers save money by offering benefits tailored to employee needs.

PFF Bank & Trust included pretax choices of medical, dental, vision, life, accidental death, paid time off, and health care spending in its pretax offerings, and long-term disability, spouse and dependent insurance, long-term care insurance, and legal assistance in its others choices. Employees were given benefit dollars to spend based on things like age and salary, plus an amount equal to forty hours of paid time off at their salary level. They used these dollars to create the benefit plan that best met their needs.[2]

This brings up the second dilemma: who should receive which parts of the employment deal? Letting employees buy benefits from a menu is one way to tailor employment offerings. Virtually every aspect of employment might conceivably be tailored to employees. At one extreme, offering a customized deal to every employee might maximize employee satisfaction, but at a high cost. At the other extreme, creating a single standardized employment offer yields economies of scale and avoids administrative chaos, but a single deal can miss opportunities to attract, retain, and motivate vital employee groups that have unique needs. Author Denise Rousseau explains:

> In a world where new services and products are created every day, individuals can easily come to value things for which employers have no set policies—from traveling to France from the Netherlands each Thursday night to attend a weekend executive program to the opportunity for an employer to spin off part of a firm's training function into a profit-generating subsidiary. Employer responses to such questions aren't readily standardized. The saying "separate but equal never is" underscores the problem of how to treat people

fairly when they value different kinds of flexibility—more still when what they want is subject to change.[3]

The right answer usually lies somewhere between the two extremes, but how can HR leaders and their stakeholders decide? Can HR leaders and stakeholders uncover the trade-offs that suggest optimal solutions, and do it in a way that can be understood and communicated? Lacking a logical tool to use in answering these questions, some leaders make unique deals to attract and retain vital capabilities, and others agree to special arrangements to placate employees (dubbed by Rousseau an "iDeal" or "individual" deal). The squeaky wheel gets the grease.

Organization leaders and executives need a firm foundation, supplied by HR, to help them understand the value of standardization in the face of special demands and customization even when it's disruptive, and they need a logical way of explaining the policy to employees. Lacking such a framework, HR and its stakeholders miss opportunities and fail to share accountability.

HR has many of the raw materials to build such a framework. HR surveys employee preferences and engagement, studies what applicants want, tracks generational trends, and often has detailed information for defining talent segments by demographics, performance, and a host of other attributes. HR also has information on how much it costs to deploy alternative employment arrangements and what it takes to customize them. The ideal tool would uncover talent segments based on the patterns of preferences, combine them with data on how employment features affect vital behaviors, and use that information to balance customization and standardization.

These dilemmas are not unique to strategic talent supply planning. The same thing happens in marketing. Increasingly, consumers expect everything from entertainment to personal products to be tailored to individual desires, and thus marketing has significant experience in parsing consumer behavior and preferences in great detail. "Mass marketing" has become "mass customization."

That principle applies, for example, to entertainment. In 1980, more than 90 percent of U.S. television viewers were tuned to one of the three major broadcast networks (ABC, CBS, or NBC). By 2005, the average combined prime-time share of the three networks had fallen to 32 percent.[4] In 1980 U.S. homes had an average of ten available television channels, whereas in 2004 cable subscribers had as many as ninety channels.[5] And mass customization isn't limited to TV content. Every minute, ten hours' worth of video is uploaded to YouTube.com, and viewers can select among hundreds of millions of videos at any moment. YouTube "partners" create their own "channels" that are viewed by tens of thousands of visitors, with no television network involved.[6]

Market segmentation and optimization have a long history. *Farm Journal*, the largest national U.S. farm magazine, was first published in 1877 and now publishes "well over 1,000 different versions of an issue based on readers' interests."[7] In 1982, the publication "became the first magazine in history to bind its issues electronically, thus customizing magazines based on readers' crops, livestock, size, and region. The May 1984 issue, for example, had 8,896 different versions."[8] International hotel chain Marriott has various subbrands, such as J.W. Marriott, Courtyard, Renaissance, Fairfield, and Residence Inn, each designed to optimally complement the others by aiming at precise customer groups based on their tastes, preferences, spending habits, demographics, and other factors. Air Canada has introduced four subbranded airlines, including Jetz (a premium charter jet service), Tango (no frills, long-haul service), and Zip (low-fare, short-haul service).[9]

These examples are not random. They do not offer every customer her own individual deal, nor do they overstandardize when customization pays off. How can your organization operate at the same level of sophistication by combining HR information with lessons and tools from marketing?

Current HR Tools to Map Talent Preferences

Organizations often use a wide variety of data and tools to determine the preferences of their applicants and workers and to understand how they may respond to changes in work arrangements. Let's look at a few of them.

Tracking Usage Patterns

HR systems can track which employees choose benefits such as tuition assistance, enhanced medical or dental care, domestic partner health care, development opportunities, training, and even access to coaches or mentors. Recruiters or search firms interview applicants about which offerings they value. Employees who are leaving undergo exit interviews to identify what made them leave.

Some organizations refer to their *employment brand* and use tools adapted from marketing to identify the imagery or attributes applicants associate with the organization. Companies may connect their employment brand with their product or service brand. If a pharmaceutical company is seen as reliable and health conscious, for example, HR might be asked to develop offerings and communications that create a reliable and health-conscious employment relationship.

These tools can tell you a lot about which employment features are used and what employees and applicants say is attractive to them. However, they can leave vital questions unanswered. For example, knowing that employees are taking advantage of outside classes does not reveal whether offering more outside classes would increase retention or performance, and it may not reveal the categories of employees or applicants for whom such classes make the greatest difference. Mirroring product brand features ("fun," "innovative," "health-conscious") in the employment deal, or assuming that employees respond to such things the way consumers do, is a good start, but it can still miss important opportunities to more precisely target the employment deal.

Estimating the ROI of Individual HR Programs

Beyond describing which employment features are actually used by employees or applicants, organizations can connect investments in those features to organizational outcomes. SAS Institute, for example, is widely and appropriately touted as an example of an organization that offers unique and generous benefits to its employees, including an on-site 7,500-square-foot medical facility and a full-time indemnity health plan. SAS also provides on-site Montessori day care. Cascio and Boudreau describe how SAS Institute can show the payoff from investing in day care in terms of lower employee turnover, and thus greater learning and client familiarity, which might be worth more than $15 million per year to the firm.[10]

Being able to calculate the employee response to employment features opens the door to even more interesting questions. Some SAS employees do not have children and don't benefit from the day care center. If childless SAS employees have pets and want an on-site pet care facility, should SAS offer that benefit? Each benefit might pay off when considered individually, but is the combination really better than offering only one or the other? What is the value of offering one, the other, or both in reduced turnover, increased attraction, or better performance, and how does that value vary across employee groups?

Using Demographics to Explain Preferences

Tamara Erickson has developed several summary profiles of generational groups. "Traditionalists," born between 1928 and 1945, have experienced "shaping events" including the first manned space flight, the Cuban missile crisis, and economic prosperity and have developed values such as respect for authority and hierarchy, loyalty to institutions, reliance on rules and conformity, and being motivated by financial rewards and security. "Boomers," born between 1946 and 1965, have shaping events such as the Vietnam war, assassinations of leaders like John F. Kennedy, the civil rights movement, and the Watergate scandal and tend to have values such as distrust of authority, idealism, motivation to change the world, and competition (because there were always so many of them going after the same things). Members of "Generation X," born between 1966 and 1980, have shaping events such as the end of the cold war, rising divorce rates, first-time working mothers, unemployed parents, and the Internet and have values and behaviors such as being self-reliant, anti-institutional, rule-morphing, tribal, and information rich. "Generation Y," born between 1980 and 2000, have shaping events such as the 9/11 attacks, global warming, AIDS, ubiquitous technology, and the most pro-child culture in U.S. history and have values like confidence and self-esteem, impatience, education and goal orientation, social consciousness, tolerance, parallel thinking and multitasking, and family centeredness.[11]

Such categories offer useful clues about how employment features may be valued by age groups. Virtually every organization now considers how to adjust or fit its employment features to account for generational differences, but for which generations? How much customization is optimal? Can generational information be combined with information about preferences, performance, engagement, and turnover to target the vital segments? As you'll see later, this is exactly what Ameriprise Financial did.

Using Market Segmentation to Retool Talent Planning

Like HR, marketing has a vast amount and variety of information on consumers, including demographics, survey data, and focus groups. Marketing and consumer research look for groups that are likely to respond similarly to specific offerings or marketing efforts. Consumer researchers also predict how consumers are likely to respond to product features or marketing. The combination allows marketing to go beyond consumer categories to provide information on both the size of groups and their responsiveness to various features. That is the key to optimizing investments.

Using Market Tools to Define Talent Segments

Market segments are most promising when they have several characteristics: identifiability, substantiality, accessibility, stability, responsiveness and actionability.[12]

- *Identifiability* is the degree of ease in describing the segment as a distinct group using vital attributes.

- *Substantiality* is the size and potential impact of the segment on profitability, with technology increasingly making smaller segments profitable by reducing access costs.

- *Accessibility* is the degree to which an organization can reach the segment through communication, promotion, and distribution.

- *Responsiveness* is the predictability, uniqueness, and strength of the response by individuals in the segment.

- *Stability* is the length of time that members of the segment will keep responding and whether it's long enough to justify implementing the strategy.

- *Actionability* is the degree to which the actions taken to satisfy those in the segment are feasible and consistent with the organization's goals, values, and competencies.

How might this framework help you set priorities for talent groups (applicants, potential applicants, employees of competitors, current employees, retiring employees, etc.)? Consider the example of Lincoln Electric. The U.S. multinational leader in welding and cutting products had a successful employment arrangement in North America based on strong individual incentives and accountability. Moving into global markets, however, Lincoln Electric encountered applicant populations (talent segments) that were more unionized and accustomed to less-aggressive employment features. For that reason, the company thought it might be better off identifying talent segments that would respond well to its practices rather than try to reach applicant segments that would require significant changes to its approach.[13]

In countries or regions having a history of collective cultures, such as Japan—where Lincoln Electric planned to expand—older generations may prefer strong guarantees of employment, significant attention to the worker's ability to save face when provided with feedback, and a more collective and less individual approach to goal setting and evaluation. This talent segment is identifiable by its generational category and employment history. It is substantial because it contains a large and productive group, accessible because it is attuned to employment messages, and responsive because these individuals typically react positively to targeted employment features, and stable in that it represents a mature workforce. Yet for Lincoln Electric this segment might not be actionable, because it would require too large a change in Lincoln Electric's traditional values and processes.

Using Conjoint Analysis to Retool Talent Supply Planning

HR tools often fall into one of three categories.

- They categorize employees or applicants by their demographic characteristics, lifestyle needs, or other factors.

- They measure individual preferences for employment features.

- They describe the payoff from particular employment features.

Marketing puts these categories together. One marketing tool for this purpose is conjoint analysis, which shows how marketing insights can be used to retool HR information so that HR and its stakeholders can better collaborate on data-driven decisions about influencing talent supply.

Conjoint analysis sees products and services as combinations of attributes. For example, credit cards have attributes such as interest rates, annual fees, credit limits, the ability to put your picture on the card, and the reputation of the issuing company. Personal computers have attributes such as monitor size and refresh rate,

Using Interactive Social Network Analysis

Increasingly, marketers are defining customer segments by using customers' patterns of interaction in social networks. Millions of tweets, e-mails, blogs, and text messages add up to patterns that can identify which individuals and groups tend to be influential purveyors of trend-creating preferences and which ones lie on the periphery. Popular tools for mapping such networks are diagrams that mathematically analyze the patterns of information movement and graphically show where the strong or frequent connections lie, mapping people according to the social groups to which they are most connected.

In marketing, the idea is to identify which individuals or groups tend to communicate a lot, which ones tend to be the senders of information that numerous others seek out, and which ones tend to be receivers of information from numerous others. Such tools are proving valuable in mapping the workforce as well.

> The chart looks like colorful pop-art doughnuts flying through space. Each circle represents an employee in an Internet company, with those who generate or transmit valuable information portrayed as large and dark-colored. And the others? "On a relative scale, they don't add a hell of a lot," says Elizabeth Charnock, chief executive of Cataphora, the Redwood City (Calif.) company that carried out the study for a client.[a]

Organizations as diverse as Bell Canada, IBM, Raytheon, and Applebee's restaurants have conducted workshops and studies to map not only how individuals share information but also where they have strong friendship ties, and which individuals bring energy to their encounters.[b] Such networks often reveal patterns of influence, knowledge, and authority that differ markedly from the traditional organization charts often used to capture organizational relationships.

From a marketing perspective, clusters of employees, applicants, or even outside contacts can be created based on how people behave in the networks. Some may be *brokers*, who exist as links between groups; *central connectors*, who form the nucleus of tightly connected groups (such as technical experts; long-tenured, experienced leaders, etc.); and others may be *peripheral players*, who seem to exist on the periphery of the network.[c] The same logic that maps networks of consumers—to determine how a message may be transmitted by opinion leaders or which groups are likely to hold similar views or tastes—can be applied to talent management. Both are special cases of customer segmentation, in this case supported by sophisticated network mapping tools.

a. Stephen Baker, "Data Mining Moves to Human Resources," *BusinessWeek*, March 12, 2009, http://www.businessweek.com/magazine/content/09_12/b4124046224092.htm?chan=top+news_top+news+index+-+temp_top+story.

b. Jennifer Reingold and Jia Lynn Yang, "The Hidden Workplace," *Fortune,* July 18, 2007, http://money.cnn.com/magazines/fortune/fortune_archive/2007/07/23/100135706/index.htm.

c. Rob Cross of the University of Virginia provides an excellent set of applications and examples at http://www.robcross.org/network_resources.htm.

keyboard look and feel, operating system vulnerability to viruses, and the reputation and hipness of the computer brand. Providers of legal services have attributes such as litigation experience, globally available offices, partners who are former regulators, online resources, and so on.

In making real decisions, consumers don't choose attributes separately. Rather, they choose between products and services that offer combinations of the attributes. One way to find out what people prefer is to ask them directly which attributes are most important to them. The problem is that people often say, "I'd like to have all the features at the lowest price." This preference is logical but not very helpful in optimizing product design.

Also, actual decisions often reveal things that consumers might not be aware of or might be reluctant to admit. For example, people may be reluctant to admit, or might be unaware, that low price is their most important consideration, but faced with a set of alternatives, their choices can reveal that low price actually drives their choices.

Conjoint analysis provides people with actual choices between products made up of various feature combinations. It can calculate the importance of features based on the choices, and it can do this for individuals or whole groups. Thus, conjoint analysis accurately reveals individual preferences by focusing on real product features and showing how consumers trade-off among them. It can then define customer segments by combining people who have similar preferences.

Using Conjoint Analysis to Optimize Total Rewards at Microsoft

As the dot-com boom was waning, companies like Microsoft were rethinking their traditional reliance on stock options and other equity-based rewards.[14] In an interview for *Fast Company*, Microsoft's Steve Ballmer put it this way: "We're spending much more time focusing on the quality of the job. We're thinking hard about how to keep jobs big and full of impact. That's the key: doing more than just fixating on compensation."[15]

Microsoft's HR and total rewards leaders worked with Towers Perrin to apply conjoint analysis. The goal was to explore a comprehensive total rewards strategy that not only would better accommodate the preferences of Microsoft's employees but also would be administratively practical by helping Microsoft optimize where it customized and where it standardized. Microsoft planners hoped to understand where investing in rewards would create the greatest benefit in employee commitment and retention.

Defining the Conjoint Design Matrix

Step 1 was to define a matrix that showed the array of rewards, and the level of each reward, that Microsoft would study. Microsoft put together a diverse team from employee research and compensation, including HR to ensure consistency with the company's other programs, and finance to ensure that cost estimates were credible and accurate. The array of rewards included such things as benefits, pay, learning, careers, and manager effectiveness. Table 3-1 shows what such a design matrix might look like.

In table 3-1, the attributes were anchored to the current situation by defining level 1 as "no change" from the current approach. This allowed Microsoft to explore not only new reward approaches but also specifically how *changes* from the status quo might affect employee outcomes.

Also, unlike product-based conjoint analysis, this analysis went beyond physical attributes to capture a wide variety of work experiences, including improved managerial effectiveness. It might be harder to provide precise costs for something like managerial effectiveness, and employees might interpret the phrase somewhat differently. But these imperfections were far less important than the need to know whether Microsoft employees valued improved managerial effectiveness highly compared to more tangible rewards.

TABLE 3-1

Total rewards conjoint design matrix

Attribute	Level 1 (low)	Level 2 (medium)	Level 3 (high)
Annual base pay	No change in current annual base pay	10% more than the current annual base pay	20% more than the current annual base pay
Internal job market	No change in current internal job market practices	You may apply to other internal positions without manager's permission	Managers are allowed to actively recruit employees from other departments
Manager effectiveness	No change in your manager's effectiveness	Organization invests to ensure that your manager is exceptional at delegating, motivating, being fair, and empowering	NA
Learning opportunities	You negotiate training opportunities with your manager (no change)	Managers are held accountable for ensuring that employees receive at least 40 hours of formal training per year	Assurance of at least 60 hours of formal training per year, plus participation in a mentoring program
Health care	You pay a total monthly health care premium between $25 and $50 for all dependent coverage	No change in the current health-care program	You receive cash for waiving portions of health care coverage

Source: Adapted from L. Allen Slade, Thomas O. Davenport, Darryl R. Roberts, and Shamir Shah, "How Microsoft Optimized Its Investment in People After the Dot-Com Era," *Journal of Organizational Excellence* 22, no. 1 (Winter 2002): 47. Reprinted with permission of John Wiley & Sons, Inc.

As in the marketing discipline, data imperfections did not stand in the way of an examination of the important questions.

An oversight group was also established, with representatives from a variety of functions, because line managers would ultimately be responsible for implementing the new rewards. Although HR pay and benefit policies might determine some of the rewards, things like managerial effectiveness and learning opportunities were determined largely through line manager decisions.

This is where retooling came in. To hold line managers accountable for making the right decisions about allocating rewards, Microsoft needed to portray the decisions in a way that line managers would accept and engage with. Microsoft's HR leaders might have presented this data in the form of reports on employee preferences or as costs and benefits of individual reward programs, but that would not give line managers information on the trade-offs and would not have been as engaging. With its similarity to Microsoft's tools for consumer research, conjoint analysis was a good fit.

Designing the Alternatives and Presentation

Steps 2 and 3 in conjoint analysis are to decide which alternatives to present and how to present them. In this case, Microsoft took advantage of computerized tools that allow *adaptive questioning*: the computer presents users with attributes to determine what is important to each individual. Then it constructs questions tailored to each individual's answers and continues to adapt as the person answers further questions.

The Response Scale: Preferences, but Also Turnover

Step 4 in conjoint analysis is to decide how surveyed employees will respond. In classic marketing research, responses often take the form of stating preferences or likelihood of purchase. What is the equivalent of a product purchase for talent? When organizations study applicants, the obvious answer is applicants' likelihood of choosing the organization. In our example, Microsoft focused on its employees and used two response scales.

First, employees answered the questions in terms of their preferences among the total reward combinations, just as in traditional marketing analysis. In addition, the final part of the survey asked employees to estimate the likelihood they would stay with the company for a specified period if they received the rewards in their preferred package. Turnover intentions are not a perfect predictor of actual turnover, but they are correlated with actual turnover. Asking about turnover intentions offered Microsoft a significant additional opportunity: the chance to connect investments in rewards with the costs of turnover and thus optimize total rewards based on projected return on investment.

Preference Strength and Talent Segments

For each total rewards element and for each individual, the analysis calculated the effect of each level of that element on preferences. The analysis also reported the average effects of each element across the full sample of employees. Some preference curves were flatter, indicating that moving from low to high made less difference, but others were steep, indicating a much greater effect. This is the same principle described in chapter 1, but here the concept is return on enhanced rewards rather than return on improved performance.

Microsoft HR leaders focused on sales and technology development employees because they were regarded as critical to the future strategy, and improved retention of this group would have great impact. In terms of the marketing criteria, this talent segment was identifiable as a coherent employee group, it was substantial in size and impact, it was accessible because employees would attend to the rewards, it was stable in that Microsoft felt these roles would be important and the employees would be valuable in the long term, and it was actionable because Microsoft had determined that it could implement these rewards for this group and in particular that leaders could provide managerial effectiveness and learning opportunities.

Recall that the final criterion for a strategic customer segment is responsiveness, and that's what the conjoint analysis was testing. The analysis would show which of the rewards, if enhanced, had the greatest chance of affecting future talent supply (in this case, retaining existing talent).

Within the sales and technology development group, the analysts examined whether preferences varied among employees having different tenure levels or different performance levels. Thus, Microsoft could combine segmentation categories such as generational differences, performance, tenure, and demographics with employee preferences to see which categories were most important in making optimum rewards decisions. When Microsoft's HR leaders engaged stakeholders, they did not present data on every possible dimension but could justify focusing on the most important ones, using a marketing tool that leaders already understood.

Reward Costs and Investments

Microsoft leaders wanted to calculate the monetary return on investments in rewards. Asking employees about the likelihood of turnover made the link possible. In collaboration with their finance colleagues, the Microsoft team estimated the cost of turnover as well as the cost of each of the reward levels in the matrix. Calculating these costs involved applying standard financial and behavioral costing methods.[16]

The payoff was that Microsoft could calculate the monetary effect of its decisions as well as identify optimum alternatives to its current approach. Borrowing principles from financial analysis, the team chose to be conservative in estimating turnover cost savings and liberal in estimating reward program cost expenditures. An example of the kind of cost data produced by the analysis is shown in table 3-2.

TABLE 3-2

Examples of turnover and reward program costs

Reward portfolio	Reward levels	Incremental cost	Turnover cost savings (assuming 1% = $2,000,000)	Net benefits
A	• Base pay: Low • Internal job market: Low • Learning opportunity: Low • Health care: Medium • Manager effectiveness: Low	$0 All levels are the same as the current situation	15% = $0 No change (same as current level)	$0
B	• Base pay: Low • Internal job market: High • Manager effectiveness: High • Learning opportunity: Low • Health care: Low	• Base pay: $0 • Job market: $1.5 million • Manager effectiveness: $2.0 million • Learning = $0 • Health care = –$5.0 million savings Total –$1.5 million added cost	15% = $0 change (same as current level)	$1.5 million ($1.5 million savings in reward cost with no change in retention)
C	• Base pay: Low • Internal job market: High • Manager effectiveness: High • Learning opportunity: Medium • Health care: Low	• Base pay: $0 • Job market: $1.5 million • Manager effectiveness: $2.0 million • Learning: $1.5 million • Health care: –$5.0 million savings Total $0	11% = $8 million savings from current level	$8 million

TABLE 3-2 (*continued*)

D	• Base pay: Medium	• Base pay: $7 million	8% = $14 million savings from current level	$6.5 million
	• Internal job market: High	• Job market: $1.5 million		
	• Manager effectiveness: High	• Manager effectiveness: $2.0 million		
	• Learning opportunity: High	• Learning: $2.0 million		
	• Health care: Low	• Health care: $5.0 million savings		
		Total $7.5 million		

Source: Adapted from L. Allen Slade, Thomas O. Davenport, Darryl R. Roberts, and Shamir Shah, "How Microsoft Optimized Its Investment in People After the Dot-Com Era," *Journal of Organizational Excellence* 22, no. 1 (Winter 2002): 50. Reprinted with permission of John Wiley & Sons, Inc.

Investments and Returns: The Efficient Frontier

In product design and consumer research, the *efficient frontier curve* shows the least costly combination of product features to achieve a certain level of sales. Each combination represents the most efficient way to achieve a certain sales level. For Microsoft, the efficient frontier curve could provide an elegant way to show which reward combinations were the lowest-cost way to achieve each level of employee retention and in a way that was familiar to Microsoft's leaders.

Figure 3-1 shows an example of an efficient frontier curve using the four portfolio options shown in table 3-2. Efficient frontier curves often take this shape, with rapidly increasing returns on the initial investments and then diminishing additional returns at higher levels of investment. In figure 3-1, portfolio A is the current reward combination, which was associated with a 15 percent turnover level. Portfolio A is set at the zero point for easier comparison.

FIGURE 3-1

Microsoft's "efficient frontier" of optimum rewards and retention

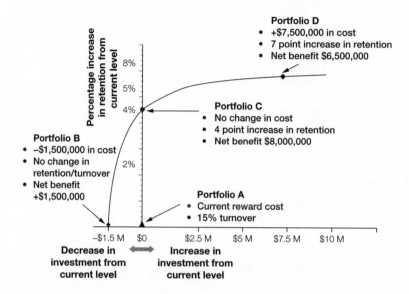

Source: Adapted from L. Allen Slade, Thomas O. Davenport, Darryl R. Roberts, and Shamir Shah, "How Microsoft Optimized Its Investment in People After the Dot-Com Era," *Journal of Organizational Excellence* 22, no. 1 (Winter 2002), 51. Reprinted with permission of John Wiley & Sons, Inc.

What did the efficient frontier tell Microsoft leaders? Portfolio B showed a total rewards combination that cost $1.5 million less than the current rewards program and achieved the same retention level. Portfolio C showed that Microsoft could keep its total rewards costs the same but alter the mix of rewards to achieve a retention level four percentage points greater, saving $8 million in turnover costs. Finally, portfolio D showed the most effective total rewards combination if Microsoft spent an additional $7.5 million. This rewards package would cause a projected increase of seven percentage points in retention. That is a higher retention level than portfolio C, but at such a high cost that its overall benefit was smaller than that of portfolio C. That's why the curve flattens out

between portfolio C and portfolio D. Portfolio C was superior because it lay at the inflection point.

Using Conjoint Analysis for Talent Segmentation

Table 3-2 and figure 3-1 show the kinds of results that can be calculated by combining all the preference results for one workforce
segment: the sales and technology development group overall. But
the preferences and the relationship between total reward investments and turnover intentions could be analyzed for each individual in the organization and then translated on an efficient frontier
graph curve like the one shown in figure 3-1. The curves could be
compared between groups by things like demographics, diversity,
generations, tenure, or performance. Statistical tools could be used
to mathematically identify how groups clustered and to create talent segments that way based only on the data.

Using such tools, HR leaders can combine employee preferences with their formidable data on employee characteristics like
demographics, and they can connect rewards cost data directly
with projected outcomes like turnover and performance. In this
way, HR leaders can retool conversations that focus on simply describing future workforce supply to conversations about what to
do to optimally influence it.

For HR stakeholders, retooling talent supply planning by using a
marketing perspective makes them more adept and accountable for
the decisions they jointly make with HR and sharpens their individual daily decisions about how to enact rewards such as managerial
effectiveness and learning opportunities. With such tools, it's clear
that holding leaders accountable for their reward decisions is no
different from holding them accountable for their decisions about
product design and marketing. Moreover, rewards decisions may
offer equally significant opportunities for competitive advantage.

These approaches to talent segmentation and preference analysis can apply beyond the area of total rewards. One scholarly study found thirty-seven studies between 1976 and 2002 that captured individual choices and preferences. The topics included applicant job choice, leader performance ratings, rewards, disciplinary decisions, and treatment of employee absences.[17]

Talent Segmentation at Ameriprise Financial

Even when HR leaders do not have data on employee preferences, often they can organize their data to reflect segmentation principles. HR systems often have information on employee performance, engagement, turnover, age, and tenure that goes unused or is misinterpreted.

Ameriprise Financial's leaders were striving to improve performance and reduce turnover by enhancing engagement and understanding generational differences. Penny Meier, VP Human Capital Strategies and Management, noticed that data had been presented on the number of workers who fell into categories based on all these variables. Yet these categories were inconsistent and were not always guided by strong logic to optimize and target the segments. Some might potentially focus on one or another generational group, because it was large or even highly vocal, while others focused on different generational groups for different reasons.

To address these problems, the Ameriprise HR leaders took a page from marketing, producing reports that combined the multiple talent attributes into a summary that better identified pivotal talent segments, clarified the necessary response, and identified the employment features the company should create at the pivot points. Figure 3-2 shows the format of the redesigned reports.

FIGURE 3-2

Ameriprise Financial talent segmentation for high-performance turnover

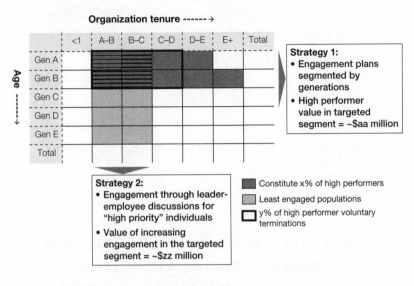

Source: Ameriprise Financial, Inc., courtesy of Mayank Jain.

In figure 3-2, the rows segment talent by generational group based on age. The columns segment talent by organizational tenure categories. The dark grey cells show the segments that contain a high percentage of high performers, generation A and generation B. The light grey cells show segments that have engagement levels less than a low average level, showing that engagement is lowest in the early years with the organization. The bold-bordered box shows the group of cells that collectively includes the highest number of high performers who voluntarily leave. The graph elegantly segments the workforce by four key variables and reveals the cells where investments to increase retention will have the most impact.

How did the segmentation help Ameriprise Financial leaders understand what to do about those sweet spots? Strategy 1 represents employment features that leaders can implement that retain generations A and B; this strategy applies to the top rows. Strategy 2 represents employment features designed to retain those who are early in their tenure, the least-engaged career stage, and applies to the left two columns. Leaders who adopt a combination of the two strategies for those talent segments in the patterned boxes are more likely to affect high-performance retention.

The potential for combining conjoint analysis with the Ameriprise Financial analysis is substantial. With preference information about the target segments, Ameriprise HR might inform leaders not only about the two strategies but also about the optimum mix of both.

How HR Leaders Can Use Market Segmentation to Retool Talent Supply Optimization

As an HR leader, you can use the following three fundamental questions from marketing and consumer research to analyze, evaluate, and communicate strategic talent supply decisions:

1. What are the vital talent segments?

2. What do we need them to do?

3. Which employment elements induce those responses at the optimum cost?

These questions offer a concise story line that connects the gap analysis that emerges from strategic workforce planning with decisions about how to invest in the talent supply to reduce those gaps. For example, HR organizations often require business-unit leaders to accommodate requests for part-time work arrangements, flexible schedules, sabbaticals, remote work arrangements, and so on. These activities are disruptive and take time, and HR's stakeholders rightfully want to know that the added effort and expense are worth it. Often, HR's response is that such activities meet a broad strategic imperative such as "retaining the aging workforce and attracting the millennials."

A more engaging conversation would present the strategic gap: "We won't have enough ready project managers in five years." Then you present the pivotal talent segments: "We need to focus on millennial generation workers and applicants, and on current project managers who will be eligible to retire." Next, you describe the response needed: "We need millennials to join at a 25 percent higher rate, stay at a 10 percent higher rate, and stay with us longer so that more of them have time to gain the needed knowledge. And we need aging project managers to postpone retirement long enough to transfer their knowledge to the younger group." Then you present the employment features and their rationale: "Research on millennials and aging workers suggests that they each value flexibility as they transition into or out of work, so we're asking you to provide flexibility so that they have the opportunity to do what we need."

In the end, the conversation is less about convincing stakeholders to do what you want, and more about inviting them to engage with the data and rationale to reach the right decision jointly with you.

You should seek out experts in consumer and market research and learn more about how they conceive, organize, and frame their analyses. Brand managers, market researchers, marketing strategists, and others can offer a wealth of insights about the right logic and language for framing insights about segmentation. That logic and language should become a part of your lexicon as they are applied to talent segmentation and supply.

You must become adept at finding multifaceted combinations of segments that hold the most promise, such as certain combinations of tenure, jobs, and work–life situations (as shown in the

Ameriprise Financial example). Today, talent supply is often segmented only on one dimension, such as "retain aging workers" or "attract Generation Y" or "increase diversity." Consumer research and segmentation usually gets more specific, and so can you.

You should invest in targeted research to precisely understand the preferences and behaviors of key talent segments, just as marketing does with key customer segments. Conjoint studies, such as those in the Microsoft example, require investments in design, implementation, analysis, and communication but can produce important insights. You should reframe such research investments using precisely the same logic that justifies market research.

How Business Leaders Can Use Market Segmentation to Retool Talent Supply Optimization

As an HR stakeholder, you should approach talent supply analysis like a strategic market analyst. You should not only encourage HR to describe things like demographics, values, needs, and lifestyle choices but also press for specific implications using the three questions listed earlier in this chapter. You should work with HR to become more adept at and accountable for identifying talent segments by asking questions: "What are the one or two key talent groups where I should focus to enhance retention?" "What do we know about their responsiveness to development opportunities versus bonuses?" You should ask more "What if . . . ?" questions and not only "What is happening?" questions.

You also need to accept accountability for your own efforts to enhance talent supply by using the insights and analysis that HR provides. Marketing analysis often reveals branding and product opportunities that require centralized consistency, just as HR analysis can reveal areas where employment arrangements should be consistent. Like marketing, such efforts are often long term and may well require investments now that will not pay off for years. HR leaders and their stakeholders should frame those decisions as they do marketing decisions, with leaders held accountable for their implementation and HR accountable for measuring the effects.

Finally, you can use these marketing frameworks as a way to recast how you define the competition for talent. Marketing and its stakeholders use these tools to identify how organizations can make unique offers that are hard for others to copy. Similarly, when talent segments and their responses are identified precisely, they can reveal opportunities to create a unique employment brand that is difficult for competitors to duplicate. That result will seldom be the product of HR or its HR stakeholders acting alone, but the tools described here make such collaborative discoveries more likely.

The tools that have long helped marketers and consumer researchers better understand and predict how customers will behave are well suited to help business leaders retool how they approach the tough choices presented by fracturing markets, the growing power of employees who control their own intellectual capital, and an increasingly diverse and global labor market. Faced with a daunting array of demands for individual deals, how should organization leaders balance mass customization against efficient standardization? Where do special deals for special talent segments make sense? What investments generate the biggest bang for the buck? How can leaders analyze their own talent to identify vital segments?

There is tremendous untapped value in exploring the connection between talent preferences and organizational offerings, along with the cost–benefit trade-offs they create. Today's HR tools provide essential insights for describing internal and external talent markets and supplies. The tools in this chapter can help organizations fit those insights together.

Opportunities to Improve HR

- Identify workforce "segments" like consumer segments, using information on engagement, demographics, performance and turnover.

- Use marketing tools to map workforce preferences the way consumer research maps consumer preferences.

- Customize features of the employment deal where they have the greatest impact.

- Use strategic workforce supply predictions to evaluate the effects of targeted offerings on specific talent segments.

Opportunities to Improve HR's Connection with Stakeholders

- Make HR stakeholders more adept and accountable for decisions about whether and where to customize the employment deal.

- Help stakeholders to identify their most important talent segments and what influences them, using proven marketing tools.

- Make HR stakeholders more adept and accountable for influencing the future supply of talent.

4

Using Inventory Optimization to Retool Talent Gap Analysis

From Turnover and Hiring to

Talent Inventory

Prior chapters looked at how to retool your strategic talent supply-and-demand goals. This chapter and the next explain how to optimize the talent flows that meet those supply-and-demand goals. HR leaders can use powerful business tools to analyze the sequential flow of raw materials to storage facilities, then into manufacturing or fabrication, then into finished goods inventory, then to distribution, then to retail inventory, and finally to consumers.

Each holding point is an inventory that can be analyzed individually, optimizing things such as shortages, surpluses, and holding and acquisition costs. This is inventory optimization, the topic of this chapter. Individual holding points link together to form supply chains that optimize costs, time, risks, quality, and quantity via decisions about how the resource moves through the chain. Finally, individual supply chains become a network of alternative pathways that can be optimized by careful combinations. Chapter 5 takes up these topics, focusing on supply-chain and logistics tools for optimizing your talent inventory.

This chapter is about questions like these: what is the appropriate amount to have on hand? What is the optimal depletion rate? What is the optimal amount to order when we replenish, and how often? How should we balance the risks of running short against the risks of having too much? These are questions that help optimize inventories.

HR and its stakeholders constantly confront analogous workforce inventory questions, even if they are not always seen that way. "Is employee turnover always bad?" "Should open jobs be filled as quickly as possible?" "Should some roles have talent surpluses, while others tolerate occasional talent shortages?" Business leaders often insist that their open requisitions be filled as quickly as possible to minimize disruptions, but HR knows that this action will mean resorting to expensive, last-minute talent sources or agreeing to expensive employment deals. The costs of acquiring talent often show up in HR budgets and not in the budgets of the leaders who insist on fast hiring. HR holds leaders accountable for reducing turnover or achieving benchmark separation levels, but leaders resist because they don't understand the logic supporting such benchmarks nor their connection to business-unit outcomes.

Organizations carry a surplus of employees in some positions to ensure that they are available, such as extra airline crews during bad weather. Yet they also tolerate employee shortages. Microsoft's Bill Gates and Steve Ballmer insisted that the company employ fewer employees than required—describing the formula as "*n* minus 1" where *n* was the number actually needed—as a way to motivate their leaders not to settle for anyone but the best, and to convey the idea that Microsoft's employees were expected to excel.[1] Is running a perpetual shortage the right way to stay competitive? Is it right for all positions?

Organization leaders are accustomed to dealing with these questions when it comes to inventories of raw materials, finished goods, and products that are in process. Leaders are accountable for decisions that affect inventory holding costs, ordering costs, and shortage and surplus risks—for example, ordering more frequently to cut holding costs, ordering a surplus to ensure against shortages, or running very lean and risking shortages. Leaders know that there is no general rule that dictates the right amount of inventory—surpluses or shortages—for all situations, so they use tools to make better decisions by logically integrating these variables. Employee separations are called *turnover* because they are like the situation where inventories turn over when they are depleted (after being sold or lost or spoiled) and then are replaced. The tools that have proved useful for managing other inventories reveal untapped potential for improved collaboration and accountability when it comes to vital questions about employee turnover, surpluses, and shortages.

The Untapped Potential of Turnover Statistics

Every HR system reports employee turnover rates: the number of employees who leave divided by the average number of employees working during some time period. The U.S. Conference Board found that 94 percent of HR leaders said they "frequently" reported voluntary turnover rates, the highest frequency of any measure.[2] Virtually every business-unit leader sees employee turnover data, often compared to typical levels, by industry, time, or job type. The Bureau of Labor Statistics reported turnover rates of about 3.6 percent between June 2008 and May 2009. Turnover rates were highest (more than 6 percent) in the construction and hospitality industries, and lowest in government jobs (less than 1.5 percent).[3]

Google developed a formula that predicts the probability that each employee will leave. The *Wall Street Journal* reported that Google's formula helps the company "get inside people's heads even before they know they might leave," said Laszlo Bock, who runs human resources for the company.[4] Ameriprise Financial has developed similar formulas and reports the probability for each individual who works for certain unit leaders in hopes of helping the managers target their retention efforts.[5]

One would think there would be a strong consensus on how leaders should interpret and use employee turnover rates. HR leaders and stakeholders usually compare turnover rates to those of the past or to a benchmark. If the current rate is higher, they try to reduce it. If it is lower, they celebrate. Leaders are often held accountable for achieving turnover rates at benchmark levels, often with incentives attached.

Yet HR leaders and their stakeholders know that managing turnover strictly to benchmark levels or past trends might not be optimum. Even a benchmark-level turnover rate can be a problem when those who are leaving are valuable and hard to replace. Matching an industry benchmark is little consolation to a leader who suffers the loss of key employees. Is the smart strategy to invest in getting turnover below benchmark levels? Should such investments be made where unit managers are most adamant, or is there a better way to analyze where reducing turnover does the greatest good?

On the other hand, high turnover is not always a problem. Leaders understandably have little patience for HR's admonishments that they reduce turnover to benchmark levels if executives perceive that departing employees are easily and quickly replaced with higher-quality workers hired from outside. This is particularly true if hiring costs show up on the HR department budget and not in the business unit. Hiring can look like a "free good" to the business unit. Yet that doesn't make high turnover necessarily the optimum decision, if the "hidden" hiring costs outweigh the value of retaining the employees who would have left.

Systems that predict and track workforce turnover are extremely valuable, and organizations like Google, Ameriprise Financial, and Walmart deserve the accolades they receive for their achievements in this arena. But elegant analysis of employee turnover patterns is clearly only one of the indicators of how workforce quantity and quality change over time. Optimal answers to questions like the ones posed at the beginning of this chapter require an integrated approach that can consider both the inflows and the outflows of talent. Turnover rates reflect the outflow, and they become even more powerful when integrated with other elements. The framework for that integration already exists in the proven tools for inventory analysis and optimization.

Turnover Cost as a Million-Dollar Opportunity

Perhaps the most popular approach to making turnover rates tangible is to attach costs to the processes of separating, hiring, and training that occur with employee departures. Experts agree that a conservative estimate of the cost of turnover is 1.5 times the average compensation of exiting employees.[6] In 2005 Walmart employed 1.8 million people worldwide. Its annual employee turnover rate was 44 percent, close to the retail industry average.

Every year, Walmart had to recruit, hire, and train more than 790,000 people to replace those who left.[7] It is a safe bet that turnover costs Walmart millions of dollars each year.

For many business leaders, the logic seems tantalizingly simple: every turnover they prevent saves the organization those turnover costs. It is true that reducing turnover cuts costs, and this logic often leads to significant investments to raise average pay, increase employee engagement, conduct exit interviews to determine employee reasons for leaving, and the like.

But let's put this in perspective. In spite of its turnover costs, Walmart's annual after-tax profits were $11.2 billion in 2006. The cost of turnover for Walmart is a large number but not a huge percentage of its profits. What level of investment would be required to create programs to reduce turnover? Is it possible that reducing turnover might require that Walmart hire candidates who stay because they have fewer alternatives, perhaps because of their lower qualifications? How would that affect employee productivity? Long-tenured employees also amass increased obligations in pension and health care coverage, so it is possible that Walmart saves money in these areas if its workforce has a shorter tenure.[8]

Cost reduction is often a dangerous goal when pursued without awareness of other effects. The HR scorecard developed by Verizon in 2001 highlighted such collateral effects.

The HR metrics showed a very low cost per hire, a very quick cycle time to fill jobs, and an average employee separation rate. On the surface nothing unusual—in fact the staffing metrics showed a high efficiency and cost control. Drilling deeper showed a high cost of training, a very high separation rate for short service employees, and declining employee satisfaction for long service employees. Further analysis revealed that six months prior a significant expense reduction effort had been put in place for this call center. HR responded to the required reduced expense by changing talent pools and reducing the investments in selection methods. This action kept costs low while bringing in applicants who were ready to start quickly but were harder to train and keep. It was a bad trade-off. It made sense to accept a longer cycle time and more cost to ensure the right person was put in the right job.[9]

Turnover Rates: Too Much Information or Not Enough?

The elegance of employee turnover reporting systems holds great promise as the basis for powerful talent inventory optimization. It is often possible to parse turnover rates according to business unit, job, tenure with the organization, performance levels, demographics, and a host of other categories. For example, data often shows that units with higher turnover rates have lower performance. Yet business leaders may be at a loss to know what to do with this abundance of data. Should they attend to the fact that younger employees leave more often than older employees? Does it matter that those with longer tenure turn over less frequently than those with shorter tenure? It is often a case of too much information, and too few frameworks to interpret the information. Organizations need to approach employee turnover strategically, just as they approach inventory turnover strategically.

Recall the example of Ameriprise Financial (in chapter 3), where HR analysts tried to help leaders navigate the various "cuts" of turnover data by presenting them with a map that showed where the high performers were least engaged, and thus most likely to leave. Departures of high performers receive more attention than departures of middle or low performers, and it may be easier to improve retention among those with low engagement. However, even this sophisticated analysis raises questions, such as how to define high performance and low engagement. Should some units hold on to even moderate performers if replacement candidates are not very good? How low does engagement need to be to make retention efforts worth the cost and effort?

If organizations hold leaders accountable for retaining workers, those leaders deserve a framework to help them answer questions like these. Data on turnover patterns has untapped potential to help leaders improve some of their most important workforce decisions if the data is embedded in the right framework.

From Turnover to Workforce Inventory

As mentioned earlier, the word *turnover* originated with inventory management. Inventory "turns over" when it is depleted (sold, stolen, spoiled, etc.) and replaced. The rate of inventory depletion is the turnover rate. Inventory management doesn't focus solely on whether depletion rates are at benchmark levels or could be reduced. Indeed, if depletion is due to profitable sales, the organization may actually want to increase it! Rather, inventory optimization integrates the depletion rate into broader questions concerning the optimum level of inventory, optimum costs of replenishing and depleting inventory, and the optimum size and frequency of shortages and surpluses.

In the same way, employee turnover is best thought of as part of a system that includes the costs and patterns of employee acquisitions, the value and quality of the workforce, and the costs and investments that affect all of them. Figure 4-1 shows that the quantity and quality of the workforce changes with the quantity and quality of employees who are acquired and lost, and that process has costs, including time, money, lost productivity, and the like.

FIGURE 4-1

Employee turnover and acquisition as workforce inventory

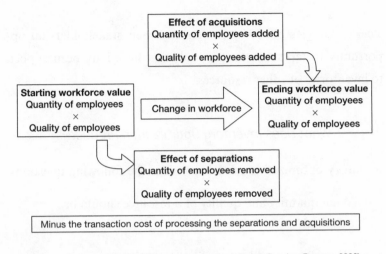

Source: Wayne F. Cascio and John W. Boudreau, *Investing in People* (London: Pearson, 2008).

I find this simple diagram useful in working with organization leaders to reframe how they approach employee separations, hiring, shortages, and surpluses. The diagram shows that if leaders consider only turnover rates and costs, they are focusing only on the two boxes shown at the bottom of figure 4-1. When their only consideration is to fill requisitions quickly, they are focusing on the quantity of employees added: only the top box.

The diagram's similarity to inventory diagrams lets leaders easily see that their decisions about workforce inventories are at least as important as their decisions about any other kind of inventory. They can also see the dangers of focusing only on one box, and they can see the additional factors they should consider if they want to optimize workforce quality, cost, shortages, and surpluses. This diagram makes it easier for leaders to see how things like turnover, time-to-fill, and hiring costs are integrated.

Using Workforce Inventory Optimization to Retool Turnover Analysis

These analogies offer HR leaders and their stakeholders an op-portunity to tap sophisticated tools that have long been applied to inventories of other resources.

What Does Inventory Optimization Produce?

Inventory optimization models consider the following questions.

- What quantity and quality of a resource should be acquired?

- How often should acquisitions take place?

- What price should be paid for the acquired resource?

- What quantity and quality of inventory will be depleted or should be created?

- What is the timing of the depletion?

- What costs should be incurred to acquire the resource?

- What costs should be incurred to hold the resource in inventory?

- What value does the resource have while it is in inventory?

- What value does the resource have when it is sold or liquidated?

- How certain or uncertain are predications about these variables?

Figure 4-2 is a basic way to depict inventory optimization models adapted to fit workforce inventory.

FIGURE 4-2

Workforce inventory analysis model

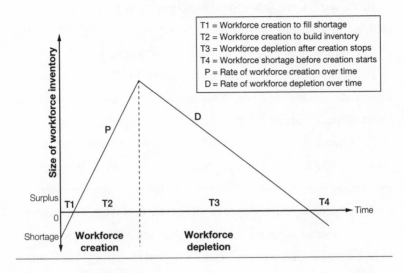

Figure 4-2 looks a bit complicated, but it is actually simple to understand. The X-axis (time) shows one inventory creation and depletion cycle. The Y-axis shows the size of the inventory. The angled lines show how inventory builds and depletes over time.

The cycle starts with a shortage (shown at the left in figure 4-2) that signals a need to add to the workforce. Then workforce creation starts when you acquire or internally produce capabilities. *Workforce creation* might mean adding employees to a job, training employees, building a pool of applicants, and the like.

During time period T1 the shortage is filled, and as a result the inventory is zero. Then workforce creation continues in time period T2, and you build up an inventory of surplus workers or capabilities, to the peak of the angled lines. The faster you acquire or develop replacements, the steeper is the rate of buildup over time (shown as P). When you stop building the workforce, during time period T3, workers leave at depletion rate D until it falls back to zero, and then it continues to fall into shortage during time period T4, and another cycle begins.

In the workforce, inventory shortages show up as vacancies or unfilled requisitions. Surpluses show up as extra available applicants, trainees, and employees awaiting assignment.

Inventory optimization involves solving for the workforce creation rates, timing, and costs that optimize the value of workforce shortages and surpluses. Inventory optimization models solve for the optimum decisions about what you can control, considering what you can't control. Inventory models can also optimize risk by considering uncertainty about depletion and creation rates.

The analogies to employee turnover are now clear. If inventory is the number of employees in a job, then the organization expects to lose employees at a certain rate from that inventory. You choose how fast and when to create or acquire employees to offset that loss, an action that creates surpluses or shortages of employees. The inventory you create may originate from external sources such as search firms, online job boards, or contractors, or it can be internally sourced through training programs, career paths that create the needed experience, and so on.

Like traditional inventory optimization tools, workforce inventory optimization also considers risk, because the rates of workforce creation and depletion are uncertain. For example, to ensure against workforce shortages, you can start creating the workforce capabilities well before the inventory reaches or falls below zero. The result is a "safety stock" of available workforce if demand spikes unexpectedly. However, depletion rates are uncertain, so this practice also increases the chances of having surplus workforce, which is the price you pay for insurance against shortages. The right question is not, "How do we alleviate workforce shortages?" In an uncertain world, that's just as impossible as striving never to have a shortage of unfinished goods. Rather, the right question is, "What is the smartest way to use workforce surpluses and short-ages to optimize risk and return?"

The most basic inventory optimization solves for how much to order and how often, assuming that prices, costs, and depletion rates are not under your control. More-sophisticated inventory optimization frameworks assume that more decision factors can be controlled. They can solve for the price you pay when you, for example, place big orders or make large production runs to get quantity discounts; the rate of inventory depletion depending on the sales price you set; the amount of money you spend to reduce theft, spoilage, and obsolescence; and a host of other combinations.

Applied to workforce analysis, these modifications can solve for how much you pay replacement workers, how much you spend on recruitment, whether you recruit large numbers or small, and whether you try to reduce the depletion rate by offering incentives for workers to stay. These are decisions that HR leaders and their stakeholders make every day, often without the benefit of proven inventory optimization approaches. Let's see how such approaches can retool typical workforce decisions.

Workforce Inventory When Depletion Is a Cost: Classic Turnover

Inventory optimization can treat depletion as a cost or a benefit. Depletion is a cost when inventories deplete due to spoilage, theft, deterioration, or obsolescence. This is the analogy to classic work-force turnover, which assumes that when workers leave the organi-zation, their value is lost. If they join a competitor or take valued clients with them, it's the same analogy, except that depletion has an even greater negative effect. Inventory analysis would attach a large cost to depletion, and optimum solutions would tend to justify spending more to cut the depletion rate or to have extra workers on hand (such as assigning two representatives to each client to reduce the chance clients will leave when reps leave). But if depletion costs aren't very high, as when low-performing workers leave and the performance loss is small, it may make sense to simply allow depletion and tolerate shortages for a while.

How can you apply this principle to workforce inventory analysis? Here's an experiment I have done with non-HR leaders. I ask them what they do when HR presents them with a 15 percent annual employee turnover rate. There is often great disagreement about the significance of turnover rates; some leaders argue that the cost of turnover is definitely worth reducing, whereas others can think of reasons it might be a good idea to tolerate turnover. The discussion almost always includes references to the cost of turnover, the lost value of those who leave, the disruption that occurs due to vacancies, and so on. Leaders' typical decision rule is to expect HR to reduce turnover to benchmark levels or to the point that operations would not be disrupted—and this without spending much of the unit manager's budget. Or, leaders will say "my operation doesn't seem to be suffering, so just leave turnover levels where they are."

At this point, I ask the business leaders to consider a different situation. What if I told them that their inventory of perishable goods was spoiling at a rate of 15 percent per year? What would their response be? Invariably, they raise a consistent and logical set of questions along these lines:

"How much does reducing spoilage cost?"

"How likely is it that we lost a sale due to the spoilage?"

"What's the profit margin on the sale that we lost due to spoilage?"

"How much does it cost to make or buy replacement product for what spoils?

"How fast can we replace what's spoiled?"

"What is the effect of spoilage reduction on the rest of the supply-chain?"

Their conclusion is that 15 percent spoilage may be higher *or lower* than optimum, and they have a consistent array of variables they would expect to apply to inventory optimization. Then I have them consider the similarities between workforce turnover and inventory turnover, using diagrams like those in figures 4-1 and 4-2. This motivates a very different discussion about the 15 percent employee turnover rate, as leaders consider the cost and quality of replacements, the trade-off between replacing quickly at a higher cost and replacing with more lead time, alternative ways to mitigate the turnover cost (such as sharing work among other employees), and so on.

Notably, leaders usually realize that the costs and disruptions they see within their unit are only one part of the larger talent supply chain, so that if they make decisions based only on their local perspective, it affects the rest of the talent pipeline, just as with other inventories. They see that their unit-level decisions about employee turnover have consequences that they may not see in their budgets. The costs of reducing turnover through enhanced employee benefits or work–life flexibility programs often show up in a corporate HR budget and not a unit budget. It's easy for leaders to behave as if such things are a free good as they request that HR invest to cut turnover. The costs of turnover, in terms of disruption, are apparent to business-unit leaders, so it may seem obvious that the benefits of turnover reduction outweigh the costs.

Reframing the discussion as an inventory optimization question gives HR and their stakeholders a way to systematically consider all the costs, just as they would consider all the costs of reducing spoilage even if some of those costs were charged to a corporate supply-chain organization and not to the business unit.

Workforce Inventory When Depletion
Is a Benefit: Training and Recruitment

Most inventory optimization systems reflect situations in which inventory is depleted by being sold. The classic models assume that how much you sell is not affected by the inventory decision. They solve for how much inventory to order and when to order it and for the optimum shortages and surpluses over the ordering–depletion cycle. More-sophisticated models can examine situations in which your decisions about how much and when you order affect the price paid, such as when you can get quantity discounts for ordering in large amounts. They can also consider how the amount of inventory you have affects the amount you sell, as when having more inventory occupying shelf space creates higher demand for your product. Do inventory models that assume depletion equals "profit" apply to workforce analysis? The answer is yes, if we consider turnover more broadly.

Workforce inventories are created in many parts of the employment process and talent life cycle. Training programs create inventories of employees having new skills or capabilities. Staffing produces inventories of job applicants, screened candidates, or future prospects. Whether or not decision makers are aware of it, they are making decisions about the size of the inventory, when to create it, and the resulting surplus or shortage against the demand for trainees, applicants, or prospects.

Like inventory optimization for goods and materials, workforce demand is more or less uncertain, so making decisions about the timing and size of things like training, recruitment, screening, and staffing can be retooled as optimizing the costs of creating the workforce ("ordering," in inventory terms), the costs of having the workforce available awaiting assignment ("holding"), and the costs of not having workers available ("shortages" or "back orders").

HR leaders seldom refer to the depletion of trainees, applicants, or prospects as turnover, but in fact the cycle of creating capabilities against anticipated demand is exactly like an inventory turnover cycle, as shown earlier in figure 4-2.

David Fairhurst, VP and chief people officer for McDonald's restaurants in Northern Europe, in 2009 was voted the most influential HR practitioner by *HR Magazine* in the United Kingdom. One thing Fairhurst is well known for is his sophisticated use of analytics to help McDonald's leaders better understand and be accountable for the quality of their talent decisions. Fairhurst invited a university study examining the performance of four hundred McDonald's restaurants in the United Kingdom. The study found that customer satisfaction levels were 20 percent higher in outlets that employed kitchen staff and managers over age sixty (the oldest was an eighty-three-year-old woman employed in Southampton).[10] Fairhurst attributed the result to the older workers' additional experience, work ethic, and face-to-face customer relations skills, along with their influence on younger workers. Customer satisfaction translates into sales and profits, so this observation is important.

This study is a marvelous example of showing the business value of an age-diverse workforce, but it also presents a workforce inventory dilemma. Fairhurst later noted that "sixty percent of McDonald's 75,000-strong workforce are under 21, while just 1,000 are aged over 60 . . . Some 140 people are recruited every day but only 1.0 to 1.5 percent of those are over 60."[11] The inventory of McDonald's older workers is quite different from that of younger workers even though the two types of workers occupy similar jobs. Traditional turnover analysis might report turnover rates by job, obscuring the difference. Yet, even if turnover rates are reported separately for over-sixty and for younger workers, how far should McDonald's go to attract and retain older versus younger workers? McDonald's added an in-store paper-based job application system to its online recruitment system to make it easier for older workers to apply. This is a great way to increase the inventory of older workers, but should McDonald's do even more? Should store managers be rewarded for building up inventories of older workers? Should McDonald's deploy its older-worker inventory differently than its younger-worker inventory? The answer is clearer when we realize that depleting the inventory of older workers can be a source of value rather than cost.

There are higher "ordering costs" to seek out and induce older workers, compared with younger workers, because older workers are rarer. The "shortage costs" of having a store without any older workers are significant, but it appears that a store may get most of the benefit by having a few older workers to serve as role models for the younger workers, so the target inventory of older workers in any store may be far lower than the target level of store employees overall. When there are multiple stores in a similar location, the value of building a surplus of older workers in one store that can be deployed to other nearby stores may be substantially greater than the value of having those positions filled with younger workers, even though they do the same job, and even if younger and older workers perform at the same level.

McDonald's should treat the inventory of older workers differently from that of younger workers. Compared with its inventory of younger workers, McDonald's should approach its inventory of older workers by implementing longer lead times, larger investments in inventory creation, a higher tolerance for surpluses and more urgency about shortages, greater use of older workers in one store as an inventory for other stores, and more careful attention to avoiding an imbalance, in which one store has lots of older workers while others have few or none.

Store managers might not have perceived these relationships using their standard employment and budgeting tools. Indeed, if they focused solely on traditional turnover measures, they probably would find that they can fill vacancies most cheaply and quickly by using younger workers, who are easier to find. This is precisely the opposite conclusion from the one revealed by following the comprehensive inventory analysis.

The inventory of older workers in one store is like traditional inventories that have value when they are "sold" to another store. The same pattern that McDonald's sees in its older workers can apply in other organizations when it comes to rare job applicants, workers who have completed training, promotion-ready candidates, or on-call contract workers. Chapter 5 returns to this idea to combine inventories into supply chains and logistics paths.

Workforce Inventory When Depletion Is Both a Benefit and a Cost: Internal Turnover

Inventory depletion can actually be both a cost and a benefit. Career systems often move employees from development roles, where they acquire certain capabilities, to target roles, where they apply those capabilities. For example, technical professionals such as engineers, doctors, or analysts are promoted from individual-contributor roles to become managers of technical teams.

For the development role—the unit that gives up the employee—promotions are like *internal turnover*, because the unit loses the value of the promoted employees when it "sells" the employee to another organizational unit. For the receiving unit, the development-unit workers are its inventory of promotion candidates. The organization turns a "profit" on the transition, and the profit depends on how much greater the value of the promotion is to the receiving unit compared with the cost to the selling unit.

Suppose vacancies among team managers are spread out over the year, and the traditional hiring pattern for the feeder pool role of technical professionals is to hire a great many after college graduation once a year. There will be a spike in the number of technical professionals, followed by constant depletion through promotions. Would it make sense to hire technical professionals into the feeder pool unit in smaller batches spread over the year, perhaps by combining college hiring with hiring of experienced workers or by offering staggered starting dates to new hires? Staggering the hiring dates would likely increase the costs of recruitment and selection as well as the chance of being out of stock of technical professionals when promotion slots open up. However, staggered hiring would lower the costs of holding a surplus of technical professionals on the payroll in the feeder pool unit while they await promotion.

Organization leaders often get such decisions wrong, because neither the leader of the feeder pool unit nor the leader of the receiving unit can analyze the complete costs and benefits. If you build up a surplus of employees in the feeder pool unit—because it reduces risk and increases value in the receiving unit—then the feeder pool unit will incur significant costs, and vice versa. An inventory framework provides a way to articulate the relative value, consider the logical considerations and alternatives, and properly assign accountability and credit to each unit, making it more likely that inventory will be optimized. This idea of interlocking inventories is an essential element of supply-chain optimization, which is discussed in chapter 5.

Workforce Inventory and the On-Demand Workforce

IBM Global Services is called the company's "on-demand workforce" because it supports the contracts IBM enters into with clients. To win contracts, IBM must guarantee that it can assemble a team having the necessary skills on time and on budget. It must balance people who may work on several projects with those working on one, and people who are needed long term versus those needed short term.

IBM doesn't know until the contract is signed precisely what the needed workforce will be. So the firm has built a system that can deliver talent on demand as contract needs arise.[12] To enable this agile supply of talent, IBM leaders draw from workforce inventories that include not only employees but also contractors. To provide a common language allowing every business in the world to describe its talent supply and demand using the same language, IBM has developed an *expertise taxonomy*, essentially making every country and job a searchable talent inventory. *Talent on demand* is a term IBM uses to capture the idea of reframing the question from filling vacancies to optimizing talent availability.

A similar principle is at work at Corning. According to its HR leaders, "One of the things we learned was that we had to get better at anticipating demand, and to do that in staffing we had to move away from being 'order takers' to helping the business units figure out what they truly needed."[13] Peter Cappelli notes, "There are two ways we can be wrong: Not enough talent or too much . . . The insight comes from the fact that the costs of being wrong in each of these two directions are almost never the same."[14]

The ideas of an on-demand workforce and talent on demand are important insights that you can extend by connecting them with inventory optimization. The workforce inventory concept suggests a slightly different goal: HR leaders and their stakeholders must *optimize* the costs of being wrong against the investment in accurate predictions or faster responsiveness. They do that by making optimal decisions about building and deploying their workforce inventories.

This means that HR leaders and their stakeholders should be adept not only at reporting turnover and calculating or reducing turnover costs, but at understanding where turnover should be encouraged or permitted, and where shortages should be strategically planned for. IBM Global Services was a prime candidate for an on-demand approach, because the costs of talent shortages were very high, perhaps even the loss of million-dollar contracts. So it made sense for IBM to invest heavily in accurate predictions—and in a global workforce taxonomy that cost perhaps $100 million—to make its internal talent inventories as transparent and accessible as possible.[15] We will return to this in chapter 5.

In terms of inventory optimization, this was a huge investment in reducing uncertainty about inventory depletion rates, creating multiple inventory sources, and holding inventory surpluses in the form of contractors and internal employees. Not every workforce inventory situation calls for such investments. Should you adopt a system like IBM's? A workforce inventory framework helps you avoid simply copying fascinating ideas and lets you know when they make sense for others but not for you, or when they are investments you should make.

How HR Leaders Can Use Workforce Inventory Optimization to Retool Turnover and Hiring

As an HR leader, you can extend your analysis of employee turnover, acquisition, and development by using proven concepts from operations management and inventory optimization. You often encounter unit managers or other stakeholders who are intent on reducing turnover costs or minimizing the disruption caused by employee shortages. You need to recast those questions in the logic of inventory analysis, shifting the question to how best to optimize shortages, surpluses, and employee turnover levels.

For example, the field of operations management summarizes inventory optimization with the following reasons to hold inventory:

- To meet anticipated highly fluctuating customer demand

- To protect against shortages

- To take advantage of quantity discounts

- To maintain independence of operations

- To smooth production requirements

- To guard against price increases

- To take advantage of order cycles

- To overcome variations in delivery times

- To guard against uncertain production schedules

- To account for the possibility of a large number of defects

- To guard against poor forecasts of customer demand[16]

The opposite conditions are reasons to hold less inventory and tolerate shortages.

You and your stakeholders can retool such questions to encourage focused discussions about employee turnover, employment shortages, and the wisdom and cost of holding buffers of employees either inside or outside the organization. Would such reductions help you meet anticipated employment fluctuations, take advantage of quantity discounts from contractors or recruiters, maintain independence of the role from external changes, overcome variation in vacancy-filling delivery times, deal with "defects" (unqualified or poorly performing employees), and the like?

In that vein, table 4-1 provides examples of translating common inventory optimization concepts into workforce inventory concepts.

Table 4-1 is only an example, but it shows how standard operations management concepts can cast HR concepts—such as the costs of recruitment, selection, and training, as well as the implications

TABLE 4-1

How operations inventory translates to workforce inventory

Inventory term	Operations management definition	Workforce inventory translation
Demand	Units depleted from inventory over time	Turnover; employee separations over time
Ordering cost	Resources needed to place an order for more inventory	Resources needed to create a program to build capability, such as recruitment, selection, training
Holding cost	Resources needed to keep an item in inventory	Resources used when extra employees are on the payroll or under contract
Shortage cost	Cost of missing a sale because of lack of inventory	Cost of a permanent lack of a needed employee (lost productivity, overtime costs, etc.)
Backorder cost	Discount given to a customer to accept a late delivery if no product is available, and extra cost of placing an emergency order	Cost of enduring a vacancy, plus the cost of placing an emergency requisition for a replacement
Safety stock	Inventory level in addition to expected demand to mitigate shortages	The number of employees or capability created in excess of expected turnover to reduce or prevent vacancies
Production rate	The rate at which inventory is added through a production process	The rate at which employees and capability can be added to the workforce through recruitment, selection, training, etc.

of employee shortages, surpluses, back-order arrangements, and depletion rates—in a different light. Even with only rough estimates of these costs and benefits, it is often possible to find areas where workforce turnover should be reduced or allowed, and where shortages and surpluses should be created. For example, suppose the holding costs of employees are low because there is useful work for them to do until they are deployed to replace departing employees. In that case, it is often better to allow high turnover and buffer it with the extra employees than to try to reduce turnover. Inventory models can help you identify precisely how much value employees need to create when they are in surplus, to offset the higher turnover rate.

The translations shown in table 4-1 can help HR leaders, HR analysts, and HR IT system designers reframe available HR information to be a more potent tool for workforce inventory management. You should seek out the experts in your organization who deal with inventory optimization. You should learn the language of inventory optimization used in your organization, perhaps beginning with a table like table 4-1, asking your own experts to revise, embellish, and extend it.

Whenever you are confronted with questions or requests from stakeholders about turnover, employment shortages, acquisition costs, separation costs, or the ways external trends will affect employee availability and separations, you should recast those questions in the language described here. Chances are that the original question will reveal a deeper question about workforce inventory optimization, along with an opportunity to engage stakeholders in seeing not only their presenting issue but also the need to consider a larger perspective. You should use inventory logic to make HR stakeholder demands to reduce turnover or employment shortages into learning moments, suggesting how they can be approached with the same rigor as other inventory questions.

How Business Leaders Can Use Workforce Inventory Optimization to Retool Turnover and Hiring

As an HR stakeholder, you should be careful not to interpret employee turnover, shortages, and disruptions too narrowly. You need to be aware that many of the costs and benefits of workforce inventory are not well reflected in your unit-level budget nor even the workforce analyses you receive or conduct. Simple rules such as "minimize high-performer separations," "keep turnover at benchmark levels," or "fill requisitions quickly" often mask important nuances when they are seen through the lens of workforce inventory. It's best to work with HR leaders and inventory experts to gain a larger perspective.

You need to become comfortable with the idea that shortages and surpluses of employees are similar to shortages and surpluses of any other inventory and should be managed strategically. If you're a unit leader, you'll find that sometimes it is your job to manage with employment shortages or surpluses to optimize the broader inventory system. Employee shortages and surpluses become something to be optimized.

For HR stakeholders, this framework changes the conversations. Table 4-2 offers a beginning by translating typical classic inventory questions into workforce turnover questions.

Few HR concepts are as frequently measured, or as misunderstood, as employee turnover. HR leaders and their stakeholders often miss significant opportunities to optimize the workforce and reduce its costs, because their decisions are driven by incomplete information about the consequences of employee separations.

TABLE 4-2

How inventory questions suggest better turnover questions

Inventory question	Turnover question
What is the optimal order quantity?	What is the optimum number of employees to acquire or build?
What is the optimum ordering cycle?	How often should we acquire, train, or develop employees?
How many orders should be placed per period?	How many times should we hire, train, or develop employees?
What is the optimum shortage to allow if we can back order?	What is the optimum employee vacancy level to allow if we can wait to hire after vacancies occur?
What is the optimal order quantity and cycle considering the lead time between ordering and receiving?	What is the optimal acquisition, training, or development quantity and cycle, considering the lead time between starting the process and having ready employees?
If our ordering costs were lower, how much more frequently should we place orders? What is the new optimal inventory level?	If the costs of acquiring and building capabilities were lower, how much more frequently would we hire, train, or develop? What would be the new optimal employee surplus or shortage?

Those consequences are clearer when employee turnover is recast as one element of workforce inventory optimization. When it comes to the workforce, HR and financial reporting systems often place accountability for some workforce turnover elements in HR (such as the costs of acquiring and building the workforce), and others with HR's stakeholders (such as the disruption caused by employee shortages or the costs of holding surplus employees). This practice produces disconnected accountability that can lead to suboptimal decisions. Retooling such systems using workforce inventory optimization holds the promise of improving those decisions.

Understanding workforce optimization often involves consideration of the links between several workforce inventories. This is where inventories become supply chains and logistics networks, topics that are taken up in chapter 5.

Opportunities to Improve HR

- Integrate hiring and retention into a workforce inventory that optimizes shortages and surpluses.

- Define "good" and "bad" workforce turnover using inventory optimization.

- Identify where talent shortages and surpluses should be reduced, but also where they should be tolerated.

- Integrate talent make-or-buy decisions to optimize workforce inventory.

Opportunities to Improve HR's Connection with Key Stakeholders

- Help stakeholders become more adept and accountable for optimizing workforce inventory, just as they strive to optimize inventories of other resources.

- Help leaders decide where to reduce and where to tolerate employee turnover.

- Help stakeholders be more adept and accountable for achieving optimum employment patterns, including optimum surpluses and shortages.

- Help stakeholders be more adept and accountable for dealing with uncertainty in the supply and demand for workers.

5

Using Workforce Logistics to Retool the Talent Life Cycle

From Mapping How People Move to

Optimizing Talent Networks

This chapter is about connecting the dots. The pathways your talent follows through its employment life cycle (attraction, joining, developing, moving, engaging, performing, and separating) potentially constitute a powerful and interconnected logistics network. With other resources such as materials, goods in process, and finished products, you have interconnected inventories that create your supply chains, and those supply chains in turn connect to form a logistics network. The workforce is similar to inventories of workforce capabilities, needs, and behaviors that start outside (in schools, job boards, other employers, etc.) and continue inside (in jobs, roles, training programs, and development assignments).

Unlike your inanimate inventories, the people who make up your workforce inventory make their own decisions about where they stay, when they move, and what they demand or require. This chapter shows that using logistics to retool HR promotes systems in which employees and applicants can clearly see positions and opportunities that fit, enrich, and interest them and thereby optimize their choices. For their part, leaders who have talent needs can easily locate available talent in the network and make good decisions about where and how to move them. Leaders who have available or surplus talent efficiently and willingly release it to other units for the greater good. Finally, the external world of recruiters, headhunters, placement services, schools, and governments is connected effectively and integrated optimally. Using better information to make better matches improves the employment relationship for everyone.

A key step on the path toward this future is to tap the tools and frameworks that have long been used to optimize and connect the pathways of other resources. Those tools reside in disciplines such as logistics, supply-chain management, and operations management.

Organizations refer to their "talent pipeline," "talent bottlenecks," and "talent on demand." This terminology is no accident, because the tools for understanding, measuring, and optimizing supply chains and logistics networks apply as well to talent and human capital. Some of these tools appear in HR and workforce systems and often are focused on the efficiency and speed of particular HR processes like recruitment or training. Yet there is vast untapped potential for HR tools and systems to be used to optimize and integrate workforce decisions if you retool your talent life cycle and strategic workforce planning to embody workforce logistics.

The Need to Retool: Disconnected Talent Inventory Decisions

Usually, leaders in the various parts of a talent system are acting rationally, based on their local considerations, but optimizing only one part of the talent flow can reduce the effectiveness of the whole system. Often HR has visibility into the whole system but lacks the tools to connect the parts in a compelling way.

Should a leader in one unit give up valuable talent to another unit? The entire idea of career paths and development depends on leaders making those decisions well, but often leaders in source units see only the costs, disruption, and lost productivity caused by this organization-induced employee turnover, and leaders in the receiving unit see only the opportunity to inexpensively acquire talent that the source unit can supply. The talent movement system can break down depending on who knows whom, who can make idiosyncratic deals, and who is good at horse trading. Or the leader who needs the talent simply goes outside the company to hire experienced employees. HR leaders are often the ones who see that such decisions carry high costs in reducing the value of internal development to meet future capability needs, but they lack a system to integrate all the considerations.

Employees, too, often initiate changes in their status. Leaders get requests every day from employees who want to join training programs, to receive special assignments, or to switch jobs or career paths to reshape themselves for new opportunities. Increasingly, an organization's ability to provide such options is one of the most important factors in the job choice decisions of candidates in fast-growing economies, but that presents leaders with the paradox of balancing demands for fast growth with demands to do more to move people along.

An example is IBM, which discovered the importance placed by employees on potential job growth.

In Poland, IBM enjoyed a favored position among technically trained job applicants because of its reputation for global development. However, because the Poland market was growing so fast, IBM's leaders there had little time to spend, and even less information available, to create development opportunities that were vital not only for retaining that workforce but for preparing them for the future. As one leader put it, "It was the transparent opportunity for learning that the Polish job candidates wanted. They were not arguing for higher pay, but for us to give them the chance to take advantage of IBM's global workforce footprint, so they could develop themselves. Development had become the vital factor in the employment deal, and it offset pay, but we had to find a way to allow folks to use the system now that the opportunities were so visible. A big lesson is that in developing countries, people are here to learn."[1]

Well-meaning IBM unit leaders might act only on what they saw locally, hold on to the talent they needed, and little realize that they were reducing talent readiness and recruiting elsewhere—all at far higher costs than justified by the short-term local performance they achieved. That's typical. HR leaders often have data showing that recruiting and development rates have fallen but can't connect those numbers to the leaders' decisions in an engaging way. Another example: hiring managers get frustrated seeing many "unqualified" applicants in their interviews, and they insist that HR leaders recruit at universities or technical schools with better reputations or at a search firm that presents only highest-quality applicants. The hiring manager sees the time saved and the higher-quality candidates recruited and considers the staffing system to be a success.

But if the higher-quality sources carry higher costs, then those costs of attracting the higher-quality candidates may exceed the cost of having hiring managers use their skills to find the diamonds in the rough among candidates using less-expensive sources. Each party in the system is doing his job, and everyone is acting rationally according to the way he experiences the costs and benefits. Yet the results are often not optimal and even contentious. *Logistics systems* may offer clues to a solution. Such systems routinely present the leaders at all stages of a logistics network with information about the overall costs and effects, holding leaders more accountable and making them better at the decisions.

Of course, the same human tendencies exist when it comes to logistics and supply chains. Leaders in units upstream in the supply chain, such as manufacturing, can also choose to hold surplus or very little inventory. Holding surpluses adds costs to manufacturing but increases revenue for the selling units down the line by helping them meet orders. Holding only a little inventory cuts the costs of manufacturing but reduces the revenue of the sales unit down the line by creating shortages. The lessons of chapter 4 become even more complicated and yet also more powerful when they are interconnected. Figure 5-1 is a typical operations management diagram of a logistics network.

The workforce equivalent of this diagram might include external talent sources such as countries and governments producing talent populations; the workers in turn move to "production facilities" such as training organizations, universities, and other employers; then workers move to "distribution centers" such as job boards, search firm databases, and internal recruitment databases; then they move to "warehouses" such as organizational rotation programs, and then they join business units that serve customers. The line between "customer" and "company" for talent might be the boundary between the employer and the outside labor market.

FIGURE 5-1

Logistics optimizes a network of inventories and supply chains

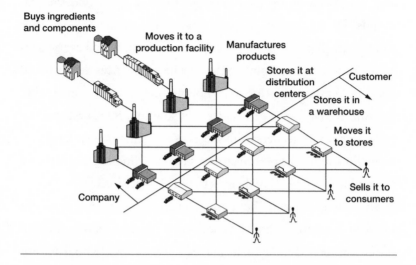

Another talent-focused version of this diagram might have internal talent sources as holding points, starting with entry-level jobs at the left and proceeding through training programs, special projects, development assignments, and ultimately a capstone career role. The details of the metaphor are less important than the logic: talent optimization involves the same structure as supply chains and logistics for other resources. This chapter shows the important implications of this simple realization.

Seen this way, talent networks are complicated. Yet the logic and tools of logistics and supply-chain optimization routinely enable leaders to manage and optimize networks of thousands of products and hundreds of holding points. Indeed, companies like Procter & Gamble have systems that (1) organize hundreds of suppliers into "expressive competition" by providing software to capture their capabilities, preferences, and costs and then (2) allocate purchases among them.[2] Why not approach the many sources of talent with similar logic? That power is available to HR leaders and their stakeholders as well.

Guiding Questions from Logistics and
Supply-Chain Optimization

Logistics and supply-chain frameworks reflect four fundamental activities: (1) planning and forecasting, (2) producing and acquiring, (3) distributing, and (4) holding inventory. The inventory optimization framework of chapter 4 is the foundation of the "holding" part of the logistics framework.

These four activities describe the supply chain as interconnected holding points that create pathways to meet demand. HR leaders and stakeholders can use these holding points as the foundation for thinking differently about talent. For example, my graduate students once did a project with a multichain retailer that often had multiple stores in a single mall, each selling one of its brands. The stores kept their own records of applicants, and there was no system for sharing them. It was not unusual for one store to have applicants who were good candidates for another store in the same mall, but neither store knew it. At first, the students' case study appeared to be about fixing talent shortages in a particular store, by increasing recruiting, but soon it became clear that it was a distribution problem.

Logistics frameworks also tend to focus on common performance criteria for each part of the logistics network and for the network as a whole. They measure and track the *quantity*, *quality*, *cost*, and *timing* of movements through the network, along with the *variation* in those four things. An ideal order is one that is the right quantity and quality, at a cost at or below target, and on time, with low variation (risk). Obviously, these four categories (quantity, quality, cost, and timing) can encompass a vast set of measures, but the elegance of these categories makes them understandable. Logistics optimizes trade-offs among these factors throughout the system. Often, HR systems already have data on these elements, and these logistics principles can give the data more impact.

Using Supply Chains to Retool Staffing

Logistics can optimize one supply chain that involves a single series of holding points, such as one set of recruitment and selection stages for job candidates, one career path, or one series of training classes. External staffing is an area where HR leaders have made the most progress in integrating HR systems with supply-chain principles.

External Staffing at Baystate Health

Baystate Health is the leading not-for-profit provider of healthcare services in western Massachusetts. Baystate Health is one of the largest health systems in New England and western Massachusetts' largest employer with 10,500 employees. Baystate Health's innovative quality and safety practices have received recognition at the highest levels. Baystate Medical Center is distinguished as a Magnet hospital by the American Nurses Credentialing Center of the American Nurses Association for excellence in nursing practice. Baystate Medical Center is also recognized as a Thomson 100 Top Hospital and 100 Top Cardiovascular Hospital and was listed among "America's Best Hospitals" in *U.S. News & World Report* in 2007, 2008, and 2009. In addition, Baystate Medical Center is named one of the nation's top 31 adult acute care hospitals for quality and safety by the Leapfrog Group and serves as a mentor hospital for the Institute for Healthcare Improvement.

Baystate HR leaders and stakeholders knew that the talent of their health care workforce was vital if the organization was to continue to achieve high-quality results. The workforce at Baystate Health and in the region was aging, and when Baystate Health first looked at its demographics in 2007, it discovered that 33 percent of the workforce was older than fifty. In addition, 40 percent of employees had fewer than five years of service, so retention was critical. Hartford, Connecticut, which competes with western Massachusetts for talent, had one of the worst statewide shortages, with a 34 percent shortfall of RNs expected in health and human services within five years.

To meet its growth plan, and given the bubble of retirements that was coming, Baystate Health needed to replace nearly half of its workforce within five years in a region already faced with shortages. In 2007, Baystate embarked on a major systemwide workforce planning effort to close the gaps.

Talent Acquisition As a Supply Chain

Baystate's problem could not be solved simply by improving individual parts of the pathway the employees followed, from being in the labor force to being a Baystate employee. Executives realized that many of the most promising places to enhance the pipeline lay far upstream, in the region's schools, employment hubs, and other employers. Planners realized they needed a strategy that would connect the dots.

They conceived of their problem in terms of a talent acquisition supply chain, like the one shown in figure 5-2. The top row of boxes (numbered 1 through 6) shows the holding points through which people pass as they become employees, and the second row of boxes (numbered 7 through 11) shows the HR practices that affect movement between the holding points. Box 12 (at the bottom of the figure) shows the standard logistics criteria that can be applied to the holding points and the ways the movement patterns change them. Baystate workforce planners looked at each of the supply-chain elements to find potential bottlenecks or opportunities.

FIGURE 5-2

Talent acquisition as a supply chain

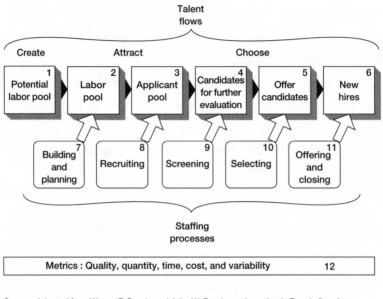

Source: Adapted from Wayne F. Cascio and John W. Boudreau, *Investing in People* (London: Pearson, 2008), 173.

The potential labor pool (box 1) for Baystate was large, containing all those in the region who might become qualified to apply for Baystate's jobs. How might Baystate increase the number and quality of talent moving from box 1 to box 2 and becoming qualified? For patient care technicians, for example, this meant getting training through external training providers. So the labor pool inventory results would show up at the training providers. Quantity, time, and cost among these training providers seemed good. Ample local training programs were graduating a great many individuals as certified nursing assistants (CNAs). It was the *quality* that fell short, because the skills being taught in the CNA program were for long-term care and not acute care.

The solution: use a two-year grant, funded by Commonwealth Corporation and the Executive Office of Labor and Workforce

Development, and team with other employers and training providers to build an acute care curriculum. One individual said, "I went from mopping floors and cleaning toilets to taking care of people on a nursing unit." One patient care technician had been a food server, and after training joined the hospital staff to whom she had been serving lunch for years.

Moving from box 2 to box 3 means getting qualified individuals to apply to Baystate. This involves traditional recruiting, but Baystate's analysis revealed that the key supply-chain element was local career centers. Baystate and its counterparts educated career center staff as specialists who became capable of linking people to the health care jobs at Baystate. This action raised the quantity and quality of applicants even before Baystate saw them.

Moving from box 3 through boxes 4 and 5 involves screening and selection, including interviews by hiring managers. One dilemma of reaching out to members of new and unusual labor pools was that managers might not be accustomed to evaluating these potential employees' backgrounds and perhaps needlessly reject them. The quality coming in was pretty good, and the trick was to not reduce it. The solution: Baystate involved hiring managers in designing outside training programs for students and selecting student candidates for them long before the trainees graduated or became applicants. The result was that hiring managers understood "where students were coming from and what curriculum they had."

Finally, Baystate addressed its own inventory of mature employees. It wanted to retain mature workers by getting a grant funded by the Commonwealth Corporation and the Executive Office of Labor and Workforce Development to study the experiences of mature workers in surgical services. The results revealed how to enhance role design with blended teaching and clinical positions, improved scheduling flexibility, and better lifting technology. The idea was to prevent inventory turnover from the final supply-chain destination.

Addressing the staffing problem as a coordinated supply chain allowed Baystate to find new ways to move the needle and invest where the returns were greatest. It allowed planners to isolate for each pipeline element, whether the key was improving quality, quantity, cost, or variability. Quality improvement systems in HR often aim to improve the efficiency of individual HR programs. They analyze whether a recruitment program is operating at benchmark cost levels, whether hiring managers are using the interview tool, or whether candidates are happy with their experience. All these elements are potentially relevant, but in isolation they would not have solved Baystate's problem, which required looking at how the elements were coordinated.

In fact, if Baystate had simply improved individual elements out of context, it might have produced new problems. For example, simply getting more nontraditional workers to apply wouldn't help if they were rejected because the hiring managers weren't engaged in the work and adept at identifying qualifications in a nontraditional population.

It's often surprising where you can move the needle. For example, a colleague at a Silicon Valley technology company once told me that in the heyday of its recruiting, the recruitment unit built organization charts of the technical and management teams of competitors and other companies—charts that were probably more detailed than those inside the companies themselves. The technology company's supply chain reached to candidates or recommenders inside other companies.

Valero Energy: Using Petrochemical Pipeline Logistics to Measure a Talent Pipeline

Valero Energy is a $70 billion energy refining and marketing company with twenty thousand employees. According to Dan Hilbert, former manager of employment services, "Once you run talent acquisition as a supply chain, it allows you to use certain metrics that you couldn't use in a staffing function . . . We measure every single source of labor by speed, cost, and efficiency."[3] Computer-screen dashboards at Valero showed how components in the labor supply chain, such as ads placed on online job boards, were performing according to those criteria. What should the Valero dashboard include as its standards for red (repair immediately), green (optimal), and yellow (warning)? The answer came from supply-chain logic. Measures needed to reflect the pipeline holding points so that it was clear where improvements would have the greatest effect, and they needed to reflect planning, acquiring, producing, distributing, and holding in terms of quality, quantity, time, cost, and variability.

In terms of planning, Valero forecast the demand for talent by division and title three years in advance. To do that, the company analyzed five years' worth of employee data to develop equations to predict employee turnover by location, position, type, salary, tenure, and division. Then it forecast labor supply three years in advance and merged that data set with anticipated workforce needs (labor demand) for future capital projects, new systems, and services. This method allowed the company to forecast talent pipelines years in advance to meet specific talent needs, along with training programs and succession plans.

Valero entered service agreements with hiring managers (see box 6 in figure 5-2), which specified what recruiters would do in exchange for a certain level of manager cooperation. This practice created accountability for hiring managers to connect their demands regarding applicant quantity, quality, timing, and cost to the resources they were prepared to spend on enhancing the talent supply chain by cooperating with recruiters.

For each internal (Valero's HR organization) and external labor supplier (boxes 2 and 3 in figure 5-2), Valero measured cost, time, quality, efficiency, and dependability (box 12 in figure 5-2). Valero also closely tracked how recruiters spent their time, along with the number of requisitions they handled (box 8 in figure 5-2). To give leaders insight into the results and performance of the entire pipeline, Valero provided each manager with a report of measures of staffing pipeline processes and holding points color-coded green, yellow, and red.[4]

Retooling Other HR Systems as Supply Chains

Although supply-chain logic has most often been applied to talent acquisition, other HR systems can also be analyzed in this way once you know where to look.

Supply Chains in Careers and Succession

The external staffing analysis in figure 5-2 and the Baystate and Valero examples focused on the supply chain to "buy" talent from outside. Another set of supply chains involves "make" options that include internal training, mentoring, and career experiences. Here, HR and its stakeholders could engage questions like the following.

- Which succession paths create the greatest value for a given investment?

- How quickly should one unit be required to give up its talent to feed into another unit that is further down the pipeline?

- How much better or worse would it be to add outside hiring to some passages, at the cost of limiting the available spaces for successors to fill those slots as part of their development?

- What is the most efficient way to accelerate the pipeline if we foresee a significantly higher need for talent at a later stage, such as where we face an aging workforce?

Evidence suggests that HR tools for addressing such questions may often fall short. In a survey, leaders in multinational companies named the top obstacles to talent management programs delivering business value: senior managers don't spend enough high-quality time on talent management (54 percent); line managers are not sufficiently committed to people development (52 percent); organization is siloed and does not encourage constructive collaboration and sharing of resources (51 percent); and succession planning and/or resource allocation processes are not rigorous enough to match the right people to roles (39 percent). One European HR manager summed up the issue with regard to succession planning: "We do succession planning to an unbelievable degree . . . but once we do it, we don't use it. Never have we reviewed a senior vacancy and looked at the succession plan. It's almost done as just another tick in the HR box."[5]

Imagine if these statistics described logistics systems. Organization leaders would insist on improvement and would be engaged in developing the new systems. Inventory decisions are typically seen as too important to allow a 39 percent level of mismatch. Why tolerate it when it comes to talent? The good news is that career management systems are tantalizingly close to mirroring logistics frameworks if you just tap their potential.

Retooling Talent Flow Analysis Tools

Many HR systems already track the number of people moving between every job or role in the organization. These systems can be quite elegant, allowing managers or leaders literally to drill

down into a particular unit, job, or supervisor and examine the inflows and outflows of employees, seeing where they came from and
where they go. Often, a matrix shows various positions as rows and
columns, with probabilities of movement between them in the
intersecting cells.

The talent flows in these tables are exactly like the quantity of
inventory units moving around a logistics or pipeline network. In
fact, HR analysts can often use the data to run elaborate what-if
analyses that show where changing the flow pattern will generate
the greatest increase or decrease of people in different positions.
These tables have the same data and logic as logistics tables that
show how units of inventory move through warehouses, pipeline
segments, or transportation hubs. They are sometimes even translated into pictures that resemble logistics diagrams.

IBM analysts developed the template in figure 5-3 to capture
and summarize the way IBM's technical professionals move
through projects. IBM used the template to simulate how various
kinds of project schedules and unpredictability in project needs
could create talent shortages and surpluses.

Often, such tables are the sole domain of HR analysts, but if
they can be recast to reflect talent flows as a supply chain, they
offer a natural opportunity to help stakeholders better understand
and take accountability for their decisions. This practice may enable planners to address some thorny dilemmas.

For example, HR stakeholders are often eager to create diverse
leadership teams. They are often frustrated by slow progress in
this area, and that frequently motivates HR leaders to solve the
problem by implementing broad workforce initiatives to attract
and retain underrepresented minority groups. "Everyone needs to
do what it takes to improve minority-group retention and hiring
rates" is a typical well-meaning answer to a lack of diversity at
the top. Yet, not all pathways are equally effective in advancing

FIGURE 5-3

IBM's template for mapping how professionals flow among projects

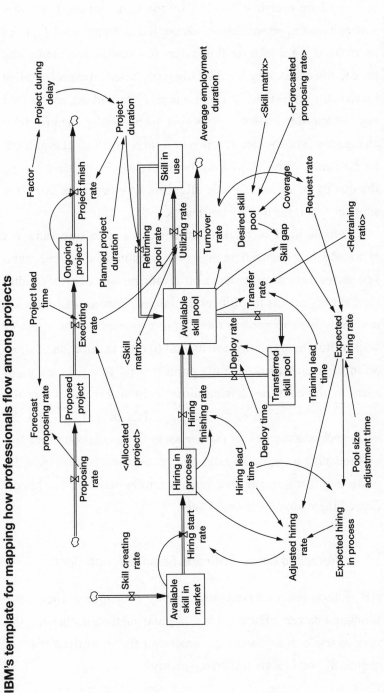

Source: Lianjun An, Jun-Juang Jeng, Young M. Lee, and Changrui Ren, "Effective Workforce Lifecycle Management Via System Dynamics Modeling and Simulation," *Proceedings of the 2007 Winter Simulation Conference,* INFORMS-SIM, http://www.informs-sim.org/wsc07papers/272.pdf.

minority group members to leadership positions, so does it make sense to have everyone improve by the same amount? A more-sophisticated approach might recast the dilemma as a logistics problem, using workforce flow tables to calculate the timing and probability of reaching the diversity goals based on expected talent movements and knowing where minority candidates are located now. Often, this analysis shows that such broad programs don't change the probabilities as much as a targeted effort at a particular bottleneck. This should not be surprising. In logistics, raising the quality of all suppliers is often not as efficient as fixing the supplier that is the quality bottleneck.

The location of such talent bottlenecks is often surprising. An HR leader in a financial services organization once told me that a key reason that women were not advancing was that they didn't receive assignments in "difficult countries" because well-meaning leaders wanted to protect them from experiencing the stress of sexism. But these countries were vital to the organization's future. So this female leader made it a point to send young female managers to the countries having more sexist teams and where the women would not know the language. Her insight was that the bottleneck was the lack of experience in these vital countries, and well-meaning attempts to hold onto young women managers, by protecting them, might raise retention rates early on, but handicapped them for advancement later.

Retooling Career Path and Bench Strength Tools

HR systems often measure how employees change as they move through a career. Figure 5-4 is a popular metaphor, showing the various levels in a leadership career and the transitions that sequentially build future leadership ability.

FIGURE 5-4

The leadership pipeline as pathways

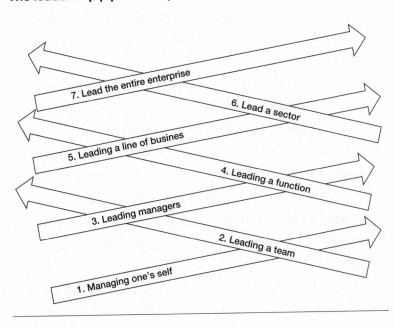

7. Lead the entire enterprise

6. Lead a sector

5. Leading a line of busines

4. Leading a function

3. Leading managers

2. Leading a team

1. Managing one's self

These systems can also consider the derailers that lead to failure. Morgan McCall and colleagues offer examples of *derailers*: early strengths that later become weaknesses (such as exceptional technical or functional expertise that later blinds an executive to the bigger picture); long-standing flaws that become salient when something changes (leaders whose abrasiveness is forgiven while they are getting great financial results but is no longer acceptable when those results cease); constant success (the belief that past success necessarily leads to future success, and failing to change or strive hard enough); and luck (being in the wrong place at the wrong time, or running afoul of the wrong person).[6]

HR leaders and stakeholders already use diagrams like figure 5-4 to discuss the flow of leaders along the pathways, the percentages of leaders who drop out at each stage, and even predicted dropout rates based on leader characteristics or derailers. Yet such information is often presented as something HR is monitoring or as a tool that HR will use to counsel individual executives. This leaves much untapped potential.

Such data can be reframed as a supply chain. Each stage in the career path is recast as an inventory of leader talent. Each inventory point and each movement between them can be measured in quality, quantity, cost, time, and variability. HR and its stakeholders decide where to remove bottlenecks, reduce depletion, or accelerate progress. The idea is to use what's already in place. HR and its stakeholders already have a logical metaphor in the path diagrams they already use, that can now be connected to the logistics metaphor.

Succession planning tools describe the workforce in terms of who is ready to step into a position if a sudden vacancy happens. These tools can be as simple as having leaders name four available successors, and as sophisticated as software that searches the workforce for those who have the right qualifications. In such systems it is not unusual for several different leaders to name the same successors to their position. This solves the local problem, because each leader has named a successor, and finished the assignment to fill in the succession chart. Yet the systemwide result makes little sense, because the same successor can't fill multiple positions.

Would two unit leaders be allowed to double-count the same inventory as committed for shipment to two different places? Logistics systems hold leaders more accountable for the decision. Recasting the succession planning process as a logistics problem captures the relationship between the bigger system and the local decisions, gives stakeholders a logical framework that supports them in being more capable, and invites a better conversation about risk, flows, and outcomes.

Getting Demand Signals Right

Logistics analysis provides an important insight: optimizing supply chains and inventories requires moving both resources *and information* in optimal ways. You can usually measure the quantity, quality, time, cost, and variability of resource movements, but the decisions that create those movements ride on information. In logistics, the information is often called a *demand signal*, referring to the idea that movements are triggered as one holding point demands inventory from another, describing their "order" using information about required quantity, quality, time, cost, and variability.

The Bullwhip Effect

When demand signals are faulty, logistics systems can lose as much as 20 percent of their value. The *bullwhip effect* happens when different parts of the supply chain have unclear information about customer demand. It works like this. Suppose your supply-chain management (SCM) system produces demand forecasts, and the sales unit produces sales forecasts based on those demand forecasts. Next, your SCM systems "stage, source, and schedule production and distribution facilities" to meet planned demand. But suppose the sales team unexpectedly increases orders because of a spike in demand. The component supplier one step up the chain orders enough raw material to meet the order for the additional components plus some extra for safety stock. They place this order with their suppliers, who also order enough to fill the order, plus some extra for safety stock. These changes will continue up the supply chain, magnifying the original small deviation from planned orders. Every successive order reflects the safety stock of all those that went before. As the spike subsides, the sales unit orders less, and that in turn translates to much smaller orders up the chain, because now the excess inventory must be depleted. "The deviations ripple through the supply chain, causing the bullwhip effect."[7]

Sound familiar? Could this ever happen with regard to the talent supply chain? Think about talent recruiting. The strategic workforce planning system (the counterpart to the SCM system in logistics) develops hiring and recruiting plans based on leader forecasts. Then hiring managers press their HR business partners to fill positions faster than planned to meet demand spikes or to use up recruiting budgets before they expire. The HR business partners convey their needs to the HR recruiting organization, and it in turn builds its own candidate inventory or places orders with headhunters and search firms, which in turn build their inventory of candidates by pressing schools or training providers to increase capacity. Then demand drops off, and everyone must unwind extra inventories of candidates, applicants, trainees, and so on. You can see how inaccurate demand signals lead to waste and high costs.

Operations management has studied the bullwhip effect for decades. It can cause very high costs and waste. "Given appropriate conditions, however, eliminating the bullwhip effect can increase product profitability by ten to thirty percent."[8] But it has solutions: (1) increase trust among the players, and allow information sharing; (2) redesign the supply chain to create faster transfers, lower inventory levels, and shorter lead times; and (3) increase cooperation and focus on optimizing across the supply chain rather than within each segment.

In the same way, talent logistics systems can move information more effectively across the supply chain. The Darden School of Business at the University of Virginia, for example, partnered with Doostang, an online job board for young professionals, in 2009. According to Reuters Online, the agreement gave Darden MBA students access to Doostang postings, which included "thousands of positions at the leading finance and investment houses, consulting firms, media companies and technology startups."[9] Doostang members also were allowed to apply directly to hiring managers, bypassing one inventory step: being stored in the online application database.

Considering the potential cost of poor or inaccurate information in the supply chain, can HR organizations use this logistics principle to design recruitment systems? Would organizations faced with spiking hiring manager requests be able to calculate the potential bullwhip effect? This capability may be important if the costs of meeting such unplanned spikes are much higher than the benefit (perhaps 10 percent to 30 percent of the value of the talent, if studies of traditional bullwhip effects apply here). Yet, to the hiring manager, much of the disruption and cost are not seen directly, because they occur in other parts of the supply chain. Investing in talent logistics systems that get better information to the participants in the talent supply chain can be costly, but perhaps it is not a bad investment if it prevents even one instance of the bullwhip effect. Let's see how IBM justified a talent logistics system that cost millions, based in part on the need for more accurate "demand signals."

IBM's Multimillion-Dollar Global Talent Expertise Taxonomy

In early 2003, IBM's top HR leaders and executives realized that to meet the demands of their globally integrated clients, they would need to more effectively move their internal inventories of workers to the locations and projects where they were needed.[10] They wanted everyone—including employees, managers, contractors, and applicants—to have clear information about changing talent needs, supplies, and ways to qualify. IBM planners realized that for the system to work, IBM's employees, job applicants, contract workers, and even its training and development assets would need to use the same definitions of their inventories of employees and capabilities. Barring such discipline, even the most sophisticated talent movement processes would not succeed. Unclear and incompatible information would cause the system to break down.

In 2003, however, like most organizations, IBM's business units, contractors, recruiters, and trainers used a mix of job descriptions, competencies, and skill inventories that were often incompatible. So IBM spent two years precisely developing a system that could dynamically define "job roles" that could span the inventory of talent and capture the specifics needed to support the right decisions. Developing the job roles meant that, for the good of the system, the various players had to give up their unique information and use the common definitions.

Randy MacDonald, senior HR officer, made this project a priority. One IBM leader said, "Randy was the 'hammer' that made it happen. He got the business units to support the use of the system, and they agreed to allow the process to define the roles, would cooperate in putting their roles and people on the system, and use it to see and find talent."[11]

Figure 5-5 shows how central the expertise inventory was. It rests at the center of all the other tools that IBM created to support the system.

Why would an executive put his personal and professional credibility on the line? The global workforce management system would require an investment of tens of millions of dollars and eventually would produce returns well in excess of its cost, but it wouldn't work unless the demand signals were right, and if everyone in the system could see them.

The raw materials for better "demand signals" when it comes to talent logistics already exist in HR systems. HR leaders often

FIGURE 5-5

IBM's expertise inventory drives a global workforce talent inventory system

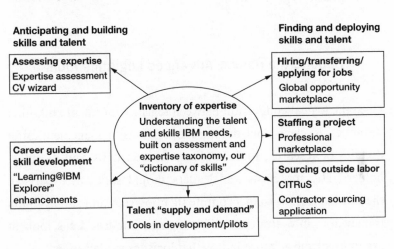

Source: Mary B. Young, *Implementing Strategic Workforce Planning*, Report #I444-09-RR (New York: Conference Board, 2009), 51.

propose comprehensive HR data systems, many of them built on a common language of competencies or skills. Yet HR stakeholders often resist the disruption and cost created by such systems. If HR wins the day, it is often because of promises to make the HR function more efficient, essentially putting the HR department on the hook to pay back the investment. Yet understanding the power of a common demand signal to create effective talent logistics systems, and potentially prevent problems like the bullwhip effect, suggests an alternative way to look at it. For IBM's leaders, the question was this: considering the billions of dollars tied up in inefficient talent movements, could they afford not to commit to the system? This was no longer an HR operations issue, but a fundamental question of strategy and necessary human capital.

The parallel to logistics is clear. Organizations maintain a common set of stock-keeping units (SKUs) for inventory, because effective inventory movement requires clear signals. When HR and its stakeholders use the right tool to make the connections clear, better decisions get made.

Beyond the Basics: Advanced Logistics Tools

Once the logical connection between logistics for talent and other resources is clear, logistics and operations management offer decades of research, tools, and experience to HR and its stake-holders. HR strategists and leaders should seek out experts in their organizations to incorporate their logistics and supply-chain frameworks into strategic talent logistics models. Let's look at examples of the advanced ideas that logistics models offer.

Dell (at the time Dell Computer Corporation) revolutionized the PC industry with its insight that PCs could be assembled to order, thus ending the tradition of building a stock of inventory waiting for orders. Supply-chain optimization provides analytical approaches and algorithms to determine when production should anticipate a flow of customer demand versus when to prepare for large spikes in demand. Techniques such as having flexible capacity, subcontracting, and multiple-product manufacturing facilities and machines are all examples of this work. Similarly, organizations can design jobs that can be performed by applicants having a wide array of qualifications (for example, by incorporating technology that offers guidance or automates key decisions) so that it can accommodate a wider array of talent suppliers. This practice is like building flexible capacity and machines. HR leaders can also create such flexibility by using contracts with suppliers and other techniques, as discussed in chapter 4.

A subfield of logistics focuses on transportation models—special cases of logistics models—for identifying the optimal placement and configuration of warehouses, routing schemes for ground and air transport, and so on. The FedEx hub-and-spoke system of air and ground shipping is an example of a business model built upon a revolutionary hub-and-spoke logistics system. It may seem incongruous to have a package travel first to the hub and then on to its destination, often covering more distance than if it had been shipped directly to the destination. Yet logistics reveals that the cost of processing packages through customs, and the efficiencies of filled trucks on the ground, is far less than the cost of direct shipping. Even though some packages move farther, the overall system optimizes both cost and effectiveness.

Talent logistics "hubs" such as centralized training or recruiting centers often appear as large overhead costs, much like a FedEx shipping hub. Yet the FedEx insight that such hubs may actually cut overall costs and increase speed and reliability suggests that talent "hubs" may also be optimal under certain circumstances. Uncovering those circumstances is easier when the analogies between human capital logistics and traditional logistics are clear. For example, many organizations now locate call centers in proximity to communities having large educational institutions and even offer desirable work schedules to attract student workers, because the educational institutions are naturally occurring talent hubs.

How HR Can Use Workforce Logistics to Retool the Talent Life Cycle

HR systems have vast stores of information on workforce quality, quantity, cost, time, and variation. These are the basic building blocks of a workforce logistics system. Leading organizations like Valero Energy are already recasting this information in recruitment supply chains. As an HR leader, you should do that, too, but then also consider how to recast other movement patterns in a logistics framework.

You can use logistics to illuminate where workforce decisions may be optimizing at the local level to the detriment of the larger organization. It is always tempting to agree to business-unit or leader requests for faster service, preserving the unit's talent, or requests for relief from disruptive "corporate" talent policies, but these are often symptoms of a global–local disconnect. Logistics have long proved useful in helping resolve such dilemmas.

You should seek out your counterparts in operations management and logistics and tap their expertise using analogies that compare talent decisions to resource logistics frameworks. You should make them familiar with the data HR already has—data on talent flows, quality, costs, and qualifications. Logistics experts are accustomed to building frameworks to handle complex networks and may be able to offer templates that organization leaders already use.

How Business Leaders Can Use Workforce Logistics to Retool the Talent Life Cycle

As an HR stakeholder, you should press your HR colleagues to present you with workforce logistics analyses that use the logic of your other resource logistics systems. You should also accept accountability for working with HR to connect the dots between your talent decisions and the larger system, and you should expect HR to provide data and logic that make those decisions clearer.

Retooling with logistics models can reveal instances when you face a talent decision that looks optimal for your unit but carries hidden costs in the larger logistics system. You need to take the larger perspective on talent, just as you do with decisions about the use of other resources. Such decisions can be contentious, and a lack of data and logic often makes them particularly so. As the IBM example shows, the untapped value of better decisions likely far outweighs the effort it takes to see them more clearly.

———————

The analogy between workforce movements and logistical resource movements is easy to depict (see figure 5-1, presented earlier) and yet profound. Workforce logistics has the potential to redefine many elements of HR, including the definition of strategic workforce planning, the role of functions like staffing, and the daily conversations with unit-level managers facing external and internal staffing challenges. Such decisions are often made on a case-by-case basis with little perspective on the larger implications of talent flows. Although one wrong decision might not hurt much, hundreds of such decisions each year add up, and using workforce logistics to retool the talent life cycle may make a significant difference.

Opportunities to Improve HR

- Integrate HR information cost, quality, quantity, timing and uncertainty to create synergy across the talent lifecycle.

- Use supply-chain analysis to locate and then unblock talent bottlenecks and constraints.

- Improve the connection between effectiveness of individual parts and the whole talent pipeline.

- Approach talent hoarding, blockages, sourcing, career paths, development, and retention through a common and integrated logistics perspective that focuses on optimization.

- Elevate considerations about workforce planning to the level of supply-chain and logistics planning.

- Engage your organization's logistics experts to build optimization into your strategic HR management system.

Opportunities to Improve HR's Connection with Key Stakeholders

- Help HR stakeholders become more adept and accountable for how their unit-level workforce decisions affect broader talent pipelines.

- Help HR stakeholders become more adept and accountable for optimizing talent movements, not just making them faster or more efficient.

- Give HR stakeholders data, tools, and frameworks to optimally address their talent shortages and surpluses, using the same logic they use for other resources.

- Show HR stakeholders why their decisions about workforce movements are as impactful and as tractable as their decisions about logistics and supply chains.

6

Retooled HR: From Risk-Minimizing Administrator to Risk-Optimizing Partner

Making Organizations More Adept
and Accountable for Talent

Undoubtedly, the work that leaders do when it comes to talent decisions and processes is valuable, so why is HR still struggling with its identity after over 50 years of progress? Will we soon see another business article titled "Why We Hate HR" or "Big Hat, No Cattle" that describes the paradox of how HR and its stakeholders can work diligently, accomplish much, and still wonder whether they are having the greatest potential effect on their organizations' success, and how to measure it? An engineer might speculate that this is what happens when well-meaning and diligent efforts are invested in a system, but not where they make the biggest difference to the firm's larger success.

This is exactly what happens if a manufacturing manager mistakenly tries to maximize machine utilization by feeding lots of raw materials into the system, only to pile up half-finished goods in front of the one machine that was the bottleneck. Operations management systems help leaders more clearly see when it is better to run most of the machines at less than capacity, and work on raising the capacity of the one machine that really matters—the bottleneck. Operations engineering frameworks help leaders become more adept about such decisions, so they can be held accountable for solving such paradoxes. All leaders are expected to understand the idea of a bottleneck, and act appropriately. They are expected to know to call on their operations management experts for help, and those experts know their job is to make the unit leaders smarter and more effective.

No one intentionally tries to unbalance manufacturing. That kind of misallocation of investments happens when smart and well-meaning people respond to the best signals they have, but those signals are faulty. When the line of sight to the larger issues is fuzzy, it's easy to believe you are getting a lot done when you are actually not, or that you are helping when you are actually causing harm. The disciplines of logistics, manufacturing, marketing, finance, and operations, and their stakeholders have developed frameworks to make decision makers more accountable and more adept.

The analogies hold great promise to retool HR. Like the machine bottleneck, HR leaders and their counterparts often make well meaning efforts to improve worker performance by setting tough goals on all the key performance indicators for a job, or by striving to meet the seemingly laudable goal of "having top performers in every role." That is the same thing as saying, "Have all of our machines running at full capacity." In the same way, improving worker performance is not equally valuable everywhere, and trying to improve everything takes up resources that could have been targeted to where performance matters most. Decisions about performance improvements for workers are not that different from decisions about performance improvements in manufacturing. Why not expect leaders to be as smart about improving worker performance where it matters most, as they would be about improving machine performance where it matters most? Why not retool HR to be the experts that leaders call for help, just as they call on experts in operations, finance, and marketing?

HR can be edgier. HR leaders can be clearer about calling attention to potentially poor leader decisions and showing how to improve them, by inviting stakeholders to approach human capital decisions using the same logic and insight they apply to other resources, with the promise of improving their focus, broadening their perspective, and identifying synergies. HR can find common ground at the intersection of proven business models and the dilemmas of talent and HR management. Throughout this book you have seen how HR frameworks, retooled using proven business logic, can help HR leaders and their stakeholders focus on what's most impactful, avoid addressing unit-level issues in ways that detract from the larger system, and optimize investments in human capital. This final chapter describes the themes and implications of this new, retooled collaboration. These themes imply new HR competencies, a new relationship between HR leaders and their stakeholders, and sources of new alliances and resources, built through new connections between HR and their counterparts in other business disciplines.

Look for the Paradoxes

Retooled HR draws analogies that reveal paradoxes that are sometimes uncomfortable: why would a leader change her hiring plan in isolation when she would never change her inventory plan without considering the rest of the pipeline? Why would leaders make talent investments to fit only one future scenario but make other resource investments by pursuing multiple scenarios? Why would leaders assume that they need top performers in every job when they don't require top performance in every product component?

Every chapter in this book poses such questions. I constructed these paradoxes carefully. They are designed to present HR and its stakeholders with conundrums that are hard to ignore, and cry out for resolution. Resolving them requires HR stakeholders to reconsider a familiar HR issue through the lens of logic and tools they already accept and use.

The paradoxes were also constructed to illustrate the fundamental dilemmas addressed by the proven business tool. Often, the paradoxes reflect the reason the tools were developed in the first place. For example, conjoint analysis of consumers was developed precisely to address the dilemma of how to balance mass customization with the efficiencies of standardization in products and services. Kano analysis was developed precisely to address the dilemma that improving everything is not equally valuable. Talent decisions will systematically improve only if HR's stakeholders understand and accept their accountability and embrace the chance to be more adept by connecting the talent decision to proven business tools. The paradox is often the first step. The new HR competency is to both understand the paradoxes addressed by proven business tools, and then find the analogies to the human capital decisions that business leaders face.

Find Common Ground

Retooled HR is not about contention. Rather, it's about finding the common ground for collaboration. Retooling invites HR leaders and stakeholders to embrace the underlying *logic* of other disciplines and apply it to vital decisions about human capital. HR's stakeholders need to see human capital as their job and to be held accountable for their decisions.

Retooling also requires that HR stakeholders break the mind-set that their human capital decisions are somehow different from those regarding other resources. It requires that they unlearn the habit of thinking of HR as an administrative and cost-reducing endeavor and instead embrace the idea that risk and optimization are a fundamental part of human resources, just as they are with all other resources. It also requires that HR stakeholders realize that when they accept the idea that optimizing organizational talent is their job, that does not simply mean following the programs and practices that HR suggests. It does not simply mean making talent decisions that are "locally" beneficial. It means that they accept responsibility and accountability for finding logic and tools that make them as smart and savvy about human capital as they are about other resources.

Are business leaders better at decisions about other resources than they are at decisions about human capital? I know of no direct studies of this question, and certainly there are lots of examples of good and poor decisions in other disciplines as well as when it comes to human capital. Yet we know that business leaders are more consistently trained in the logical frameworks of other disciplines, and that those frameworks are likely to be more natural and acceptable to them, even if they don't always make the best decisions in those arenas. The common ground for collaboration rests not just in revealing the paradoxes that show that human capital decisions could be better. It also rests in having the mutual competency to start with the business logic and tools that stakeholders already understand, respect the value and power of those frameworks, and invite a partnership that applies them to a new area—talent and human capital.

R-i-s-k Is Not a Four-Letter Word in HR

Every chapter in this book deals with risk, because risk in talent management is a fact, just as it is in every other aspect of organizational decision making. Table 6-1 shows how each chapter has retooled a common misconception about risk in human resources by using proven business frameworks.

The examples in the chapters provide starting points for rethinking risk in talent management. HR decisions often emphasize risk removal rather than risk optimization. Yet, as you have seen, virtually all other management disciplines evaluate risk more objectively, optimize it, and accept it when it makes sense to do so. In the same way, risk and uncertainty about human capital are facts of organizational life, and optimizing human capital risk often provides opportunities to create a significant competitive advantage.

HR leaders and their stakeholders should reframe the conversation. Consider not only "how do we minimize or reduce risk in our human capital," but "how do we more deeply learn to understand human capital risk, optimize it, and properly enable and reward organization leaders for taking the right risks, and managing the uncertainties well."

Finding the Inflection Points

Another running theme throughout this book is the idea of inflection points. Virtually every management model you've seen has at

TABLE 6-1

Retooling HR involves rethinking the idea of risk in talent management

Chapter	Traditional HR risk framing	Business tool applied to HR	Retooled approach to talent risk
1: Retooling work analysis	"We should have top performers in every position to minimize the risk of bad performance."	Performance tolerance analysis optimizes performance improvement against risks, costs, and benefits.	"Minimize risk in risk-averse performance situations and embrace it in risk-loving performance situations by focusing on return on improved performance (ROIP)."
2: Retooling talent scenarios	"Minimize the risk of talent being unprepared for the future by developing generic competencies that will apply across the board."	Portfolio analysis balances the risks of several uncertain future scenarios against their returns, diversifying resource investments to fit several future possibilities.	"Balance risk in talent planning with diversified investments in talent for several future scenarios according to their relative likelihood and risk."
3: Retooling the talent supply strategy	"Minimize the risk of employee dissatisfaction by agreeing to customized deals, or minimize the risk of inequity by doing the same thing for everyone."	Customer segmentation optimizes product and service features to customize against market segments, according to their value and cost.	"Balance the risk of dissatisfaction or inequity against the return by customizing where it achieves the greatest return and standardizing where it does not."
4: Retooling talent shortages and surpluses	"Minimize the risk of employee shortages by filling all requisitions as quickly as possible and keeping turnover to a minimum."	Inventory management optimizes holding costs, ordering costs, and shortage costs by planning for shortages or surpluses.	"Turnover levels and time-to-fill are optimized to create the level of employee shortages or surpluses that best balances risks of surpluses and shortages against costs."
5: Retooling the talent life cycle	"Minimize risk by having successors for every position who have completed the career development path requirements."	Logistics management optimizes transport patterns to balance the risk of unavailability against the costs and returns of following various pathways.	"Optimize the risk and return of succession by balancing the costs, benefits, and timing of various career paths."

its base the idea of trade-offs. Trade-offs are inevitable and necessary. The trick is to make them in a way that strikes the optimal
balance. Chapter 1 focuses on the inflection points where performance value levels off or accelerates. It pays to invest in improving
work performance when the curve is steep (or "pivotal"), but perhaps not where the curve is flat. Chapter 2 describes how inflection
points across future scenarios define when to invest in talent to prepare for one future, multiple futures, or stay generic. The inflection
point is where the optimum investment shifts, depending on future
risks. Chapter 3 shows that what workers want and need often
defines an inflection point that indicates where organizations can
get the biggest bang for their investments in the employment deal.
In Chapter 4 we see that inventory shortage costs and holding costs
move in different directions and define inflection points where employee shortages or surpluses become strategically valuable.
Chapter 5 shows that logistics tools can reveal where supply chains
and logistics networks create inflection points in the form of bottlenecks and unused capacity, and how they help optimize the
pathways organizations use to acquire and develop human capital.

HR's stakeholders often expect HR to provide talent solutions
that achieve the best of all worlds, but the reality is that talent
decisions involve trade-offs. Other disciplines articulate this principle well, and retooling helps HR leaders and their constituents
find the trade-offs and avoid missing collateral effects. The win-
ners will make trade-offs wisely and will not ignore them or pre-
tend they do not exist.

Segmentation and Differentiation

Retooling HR taps business disciplines that recognize that some
things matter more than others. The value of differentiation is

fundamental. Chapter 1 applies this idea to the demand side of workforce planning, showing that even something as valuable as performance is not equally valuable everywhere. Chapter 3 applies this principle to the supply side of workforce planning, extending the classic idea of customer segments to employee segments based on how individuals respond to the employment deal. It shows that marketing tools can reveal how to make the deal more nuanced and more powerful. Rewards and their combinations yield curves like those shown in chapter 1. Differentiation is the antidote to generic human capital policies and programs that sound good but may fail to capitalize on vital opportunities. The fundamental principle of the 80-20 rule (that 80 percent of the effect may be caused by the 20 percent most vital parts of the system) is pervasive in management, whether considering inventories, customer segments, supply-chain elements, or production facilities. There is great value in applying this principle more explicitly to human capital. The language to guide that application rests in retooled HR frameworks like those described here. Retooling HR means shifting your focus from what's important to what's pivotal. Where does performance or rewards make the biggest difference (chapters 1 and 3)? Where will changed future scenarios reveal investment options (chapter 2)? Where do movements of talent reveal ways to optimize the entire system (chapters 4 and 5)?

Find New Allies

What do operations engineers, marketing researchers, portfolio managers, and logistics experts have to teach HR leaders? A vital message for HR leaders is to tap their colleagues who are the functional and process experts in other disciplines to build the next generation of human capital optimization tools. Such tools must not be simply "HR tools" that are owned and operated by the HR function. If retooling simply makes HR leaders better, its greatest promise will have been missed. A vital goal of connecting HR decisions with proven business logic is that the tools belong to the leaders who make human capital decisions. Those leaders are often outside the HR profession. As with other professions, those leaders will rely on their HR counterparts to hold them accountable and make them more adept. A good beginning for building the credibility and legitimacy required in HR is to have functional experts from other disciplines as allies.

Another advantage of seeking out allies in other functions is that those experts can help HR leaders be smarter about the proven business models that support those functions. The examples in this book are explicitly based on classic and foundational principles, but every discipline has decades of additional research and learning. Every organization has its own unique approaches to disciplines such as consumer research, portfolio diversification, and logistics, so experts in these disciplines can help HR leaders use the right language, metaphors, and analysis approaches to maximize their relevance. The retooled HR approaches will then have both the credibility and logical sophistication to warrant ownership by savvy line leaders.

However, HR leaders should approach these experts carefully. It's better simply to ask your counterparts, "Tell me how you think about inventory," than to say, "Please develop an inventory model for my turnover problem." The first step is for HR leaders to become more competent in the frameworks of their counterparts. Then, as competence and collaborative relationships grow, it will be possible to enlist partners from other disciplines in considering the specific human capital dilemmas where their frameworks can apply. This book is designed to help HR leaders make those vital initial connections between talent decisions and these other disciplines as the first step to building richer connections, more insightful retooled HR frameworks, and more fruitful conversations.

Consider what a stranger thinks to be strange.[1] This means that strangers to the established thinking will ask naive questions or pose perspectives that seem less expert, but in fact reveal the unanswered issues that the "natives" have long ago learned to ignore. A theme of this book is to create opportunities for strangers to share their ideas. Every framework in this book is well understood by leaders in disciplines and functions that are seldom involved in HR systems and decisions. There are smart, well-meaning and motivated experts in HR and in functions such as operations, supply chain, finance, and marketing. As you've seen, some things in HR will seem strange to an engineer, a financial risk expert, or a supply-chain analyst. They may well wonder why human resources maintains rules such as "minimize talent shortages everywhere," "top performers in every role," or "four successors for every leadership position," when such rules clearly run counter to standard logic models in the other functional areas. A fundamental purpose of this book is to encourage leaders within and outside HR to listen carefully to what appears strange to each of them and to find new insights by reconciling their perspectives.

A Retooled Perspective on Strategic Planning

What if you retooled strategic HR planning to reflect the tenets of logistics, portfolio theory, and segmentation? Figure 6-1 illustrates a possible merger.

The talent life cycle, shown in figure 6-1 as the boxes farthest from the center, comprises the HR activities and processes that are the levers used by HR and its stakeholders. These activities and processes can be thought of as the holding points in a talent

FIGURE 6-1

The retooled employment life cycle

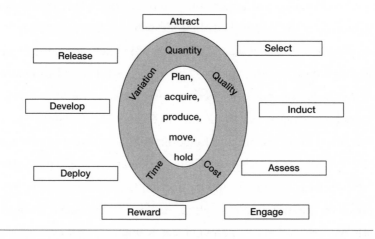

logistics network. HR systems apply the activities shown in the center, to each of the holding points around the perimeter. The metrics shown in the middle (quantity, quality, cost, time, and variation) are the measures that chapter 5 showed are fundamental to logistics, and would become fundamental to the HR strategic workforce planning system. In essence, this framework suggests that strategic workforce planning might be retooled to reflect the basic principles of inventory optimization and logistics discussed in chapters 4 and 5. This approach would combine with a more precise definition of performance inflection points described in chapter 2 as the basic language of the work. It would approach forecasting and uncertainty using risk optimization and diversification tools described in chapter 3 to pursue multiple future scenarios at once. It would then invest to induce workers to apply, join, move and develop, using the logic and data tools of consumer behavior in chapter 4.

This idea is speculative today, but it invites HR leaders and their stakeholders to consider how their planning systems might more directly incorporate the idea of workforce planning as optimizing the movements through a system, considering risk and return. It provides a metaphor that is pervasive and fundamental to other business decisions. Envisioning strategic workforce planning as optimizing human capital movements against risk, return, and cost taps the language of proven business tools, augmenting and building on the planning frameworks already used in your organization.

Innovation and Rapid Prototyping: Logic First, and Then Numbers

How many individuals would associate the words *innovation*, *play*, and *rapid prototyping* with human resource management?[2] Retooling HR requires exactly these perspectives. The business models have been around for decades, but applying them to HR is largely new and not widely accepted. HR systems are seldom obviously compatible with the proven business frameworks described here. As organizations apply these ideas they will encounter tough questions. How do you measure the "holding costs" of an employee "inventory"? How do you map the paths through the career pipeline and assign values to them that allow optimizing the flow of talent? How do you measure the ROIP curves for various roles, jobs, and competencies when your existing systems rely heavily on job descriptions?

These questions are not easily answered in many organizations, but the lack of immediate answers represents the opportunity, not the roadblock. In the history of other business disciplines, it is usually the logic that precedes the systems and the measurement, not the other way around. Well-developed supply-chain, market research, finance, and operations management databases and measures did not emerge first and then become infused later with logical models such as portfolio theory and conjoint analysis. Rather, the concepts of risk and return, portfolio theory, logistics optimization, and market segmentation came first. Organizations tested and applied those concepts, usually imperfectly, by using existing systems and data along with a good deal of speculation and estimation. However, as the power of the logic became apparent, it also revealed how to advance the systems and measures to support the new tools.

This brings us back to innovation, play, and rapid prototyping. Michael Schrage's book *Serious Play*, which chronicles how companies innovate successfully, makes the point well:

> The essence of serious play is the challenge and thrill of confronting uncertainties. Whether uncertainties are obstacles or allies depends on how you play. The challenge of converting uncertainty into manageable risks or opportunities explains why serious play is often the most rational behavior for innovators . . . Serious play is about improvising with the unanticipated in ways that create new value. Any tools, technologies, techniques or toys that let people improve how they play seriously with uncertainty is guaranteed to improve the quality of innovation.[3]

A central premise of this book is the need to confront uncertainty by playing with the logic of a well-developed framework to apply it to a talent dilemma. Virtually every chapter involves "playing seriously with uncertainty."

HR tends to be specification driven, carefully considering all the necessary elements, developing a well-vetted specification, and implementing a specified system. In contrast, a prototype-driven approach strives to get quickly to a working, and imperfect, prototype that clients can see and use. Developing a prototype means accepting the probability that clients will reject and modify it. The solution is to identify a few important design criteria and create a "quick and dirty" prototype *designed to be rejected* and seen as a vehicle for further conversation and development.[4] Imperfection is not a reason to wait.

People Aren't Numbers

Retooling HR does not dehumanize human resources. People can make choices about joining, learning, developing, and leaving organizations. They are not simply cogs in a wheel, units of inventory, investment vehicles, or logistics variables. The optimization choices suggested by retooled HR frameworks will always be tempered by the reactions and responses of the real people they affect.

Still, as the examples show, every management system has such human elements, not just HR. Supply-chain partners don't want to give up control, and as a result they experience a bullwhip effect. Consumers don't follow their preferences with perfect precision. Engineering components have variations because humans create them. Engineering designs reflect negotiation and egos as well as hard-nosed analysis. A retooled HR world will still have great need for the humanity that is the hallmark of the profession. Indeed, as you retool HR, you'll probably improve on the business tools by making them smarter about the human elements that affect them.

Uncertain human behavior does not mean random human behavior. Retooled HR means that talent decisions can start with more optimum goals, which hold substantial value not only for the decision makers but also for the employees affected by the decisions. HR strategies and designs that make better connections, fit employee preferences more optimally, and provide more transparent logic all foster a fairer and more human employment relationship. In the end, that may be the most promising result of retooling HR.

Notes

Introduction

1. Stephen Baker, "Data Mining Moves to Human Resources," *BusinessWeek*, March 12, 2009.

2. Wayne F. Cascio and John W. Boudreau, *Investing in People* (New York: Pearson, 2008).

3. Jeffrey Pfeffer, "Changing Mental Models: HR's Most Important Task," *Human Resource Management* 44, no. 2 (2005): 123–128.

4. Jeffrey Pfeffer, "Human Resources from an Organizational Behavior Perspective: Some Paradoxes Explained," *Journal of Economic Perspectives* 21, no. 4 (2007): 115–134.

5. Craig Pinder, *Work Motivation in Organizational Behavior* (New York: Psychology Press, 2008).

6. John W. Boudreau and Peter M. Ramstad, *Beyond HR: The New Science of Human Capital* (Boston: Harvard Business School Publishing, 2007), chapter 9; Cascio and Boudreau, *Investing in People*.

Chapter 1

1. John W. Boudreau and Peter M. Ramstad, *Beyond HR: The New Science of Human Capital* (Boston: Harvard Business School Publishing, 2007).

2. Ibid.

3. S. Miller, "Collaboration Is Key to Effective Outsourcing," in *2008 HR Trend Book* (Alexandria, VA: Society for Human Resource Management, 2007), 58–61.

4. Peter Sanders and Daniel Michaels, "Boeing Looks Beyond Dreamliner's First Flight," *Wall Street Journal* online, December 15, 2009.

5. Noriaki Kano, Nobuhiku Seraku, Fumio Takahashi, and Shinichi Tsuji, "Attractive Quality and Must-Be Quality," *Journal of the Japanese Society for Quality Control* 14, no. 2 (April 1984): 39–48, http://ci.nii.ac.jp/Detail/detail.do?LOCALID=ART0003570680&lang=en.

6. Thanks to Peter M. Ramstad of The Toro Company for valuable contributions to the ideas in this section.

7. Boudreau and Ramstad, *Beyond HR*.

8. Ibid.

9. Peter Sanders, "Corporate News: Boeing Sets Deal to Buy a Dreamliner Plant—Company to Pay Vought Aircraft $580 Million, Forgive Cash Advances for Work on 787," *Wall Street Journal*, July 8, 2009, B3; and Peter Sanders, "Corporate News: Boeing Takes Control of Plant," *Wall Street Journal*, December 23, 2009, B2.

10. Boudreau and Ramstad, *Beyond HR*.

11. P. W. Tam and K. J. Delaney, "Talent Search: Google's Growth Helps Ignite Silicon Valley Hiring Frenzy," *Wall Street Journal*, November 23, 2005, A1.

12. Wayne F. Cascio and John W. Boudreau, *Investing in People* (New York: Pearson, 2008).

13. Alec Levenson and Tracy Faber, "Count on Productivity Gains," *HR Magazine,* June 2009, 70.

14. Ibid., 74.

15. Cascio and Boudreau, *Investing in People*.

16. Peter Attfield interview with author, January 2010.

Chapter 2

1. Michael Patsualos-Fox, Dennis Carey, and Michael Useem, "Leadership Lessons for Hard Times," *McKinsey Quarterly*, July 2009, 1.

2. Thomas J. Chermack and Richard Swanson, "Scenario Planning: Human Resource Development's Strategic Learning Tool," *Advances in Developing Human Resources* 10 (2008), http://adh.sagepub.com/cgi/content/abstract/10/2/129.

3. Author interview with Robert Calo, IBM, July 2009.

4. Mary B. Young, *Implementing Strategic Workforce Planning*, Research Working Group Report I444-09-RR (New York: Conference Board, 2009).

5. Jay A. Conger and Douglas A. Ready, "Rethinking Leadership Competencies," *Leader to Leader*, Spring 2004, 44.

6. Christine M. Riordan, "Navigating Through Leadership Transitions: Making It Past the Twists and Turns," *Ivey Business Journal* 72, no. 3 (May/June 2008), 11.

7. John R. Ryan, "Learning Agility Equals Leadership Success," *BusinessWeek*, February 27, 2009, http://www.businessweek.com/managing/content/feb2009/ca20090227_893956.htm.

8. T. Hill, *Manufacturing Strategy: Text and Cases* (Boston: McGraw Hill, 2000), 142.

9. Gopesh Anand and Peter T. Ward, "Fit, Flexibility and Performance in Manufacturing: Coping with Dynamic Environments," *Production and Operations Management* 13, no. 4 (December 1, 2004): 369–385.

10. Janet McFarland, "OPG Directors Had Talent, Sadly the Wrong Kind," December 17, 2003, http://mailman.mcmaster.ca/mailman/private/cdn-nucl-l/0312.gz/msg00049.html.

11. John Bronson, personal communication with the author, January 2010.

12. Kevin Lane and Florian Pollner, "How to Address China's Growing Talent Shortage," *McKinsey Quarterly*, March 2008, 36.

13. Personal conversation between author and HR executive at a global high-tech company, March 2009.

14. Young, *Implementing Strategic Workforce Planning*.

15. Ibid.

16. Mayank Jain, Ameriprise Financial, personal conversation, December 2009.

17. Hagen Lindstadt and Jürgen Müller, "Making Game Theory Work for Managers," *McKinsey Quarterly*, December, 2009.

18. Fay Hansen, "Strategic Workforce Planning in an Uncertain World," *Workforce Management* online, July 2009, http://www.workforce.com/section/09/feature/26/53/34/index.html.

Chapter 3

1. "Perk Place: The Benefits Offered by Google and Others May Be Grand, but They're All Business," *Knowledge@Wharton*, March 21, 2007, http://knowledge.wharton.upenn.edu/article.cfm?articleid=1690.

2. Martin Levy, "The ABC's of Cafeteria Plans," *Workspan,* June 2002.

3. Denise Rousseau, *I-Deals: Idiosyncratic Deals Employees Bargain for Themselves* (Armonk, NY: M.E. Sharpe, Inc., 2005), xi.

4. Neilsen Media Research, "Nielsen September 12–18 Ratings," *Broadcasting and Cable* 135, no. 39 (2005): 23.

5. Douglas Blanks Hindman and Kenneth Weigand, "The Big Three's Prime-Time Decline: A Technological and Social Context," *Journal of Broadcasting and Electronic Media*, March 1, 2008.

6. YouTube.com, http://www.youtube.com/t/partnerships_faq, http://www.youtube.com/t/fact_sheet.

7. Art Weinstein, *Market Segmentation*, 3rd ed. (Binghamton, NY: Hayworth Press, 2004), 3.

8. Agweb.com, February, 2010. http://www.agweb.com/FarmJournal/about/Article.aspx?ID=144158.

9. Wayne F. Cascio and John W. Boudreau, *Investing in People* (London: Pearson, 2008).

10. Cascio and Boudreau, *Investing in People.*

11. Tamara Erickson, *The New Employee-Employer Equation* (New York: nGenera (formerly BSG Concours), 2007).

12. Michel Wedel and Wagner Antonio Kamakura, *Market Segmentation: Conceptual and Methodological Foundations* (Norwell, MA: Kluwer, 2000), 4–5.

13. Christopher Bartlett and Jamie O'Connell, "Lincoln Electric: Venturing Abroad," case 398095-PDF-ENG (Boston: Harvard Business School Publishing, 1998).

14. The material in this section is based on L. Allen Slade, Thomas O. Davenport, Darryl R. Roberts, and Shamir Shah, "How Microsoft Optimized Its Investment in People after the Dot-Com Era," *Journal of Organizational Excellence* 22, no. 1 (Winter 2002): 43–52.

15. George Anders, "Steve Ballmer's Big Moves," *Fast Company*, March 2001, 148.

16. See Cascio and Boudreau, *Investing in People*, for examples of turnover costing formulas.

17. Ronald J. Karren and Melissa Woodard Barringer, "A Review and Analysis of the Policy-Capturing Methodology in Organizational Research: Guidelines for Research and Practice," *Organizational Research Methods* 5, no. 4 (2002): 337–387.

Chapter 4

1. Christopher Bartlett and Meg Wozny, "Microsoft's Human Resource Practices: Making People Strategic Assets," Case 9-300-004 (Boston: Harvard Business School Publishing, 2001), 2.

2. Stephen Gates, *Strategic Human Capital Measures*, Report R-1417-08-WG (New York: Conference Board, 2008).

3. Bureau of Labor Statistics, "Economic News Release," http://www.bls.gov/news.release/jolts.t03.htm.

4. Scott Morrison, "Google Searches for Staffing Answers," *Wall Street Journal*, May 19, 2009, B1.

5. Mayank Jain, Ameriprise Financial, personal interview with author, December 2009.

6. Wayne F. Cascio and John W. Boudreau, *Investing in People* (London: Pearson, 2008).

7. Ibid., 67.

8. Ibid.

9. Garrett Walker and J. Randall MacDonald, "Designing and Implementing an HR Scorecard," *Human Resource Management* 40, no. 4 (Winter 2001): 365–377.

10. Richard Tyler, "Workers Over 60 Are Surprise Key to McDonald's Sales," *Telegraph*, August 13, 2009, http://www.telegraph.co.uk/finance/newsbysector/retailandconsumer/6017391/Workers-over-60-are-surprise-key-to-McDonalds-sales.html.

11. Ibid.

12. Mary B. Young, *Implementing Strategic Workforce Planning*, Research Working Group Report I444-09-RR (New York: Conference Board 2009), 49–50.

13. Peter Cappelli, "A Supply Chain Approach to Workforce Planning," *Organizational Dynamics* 30, no.1 (January–March 2009): 11.

14. Ibid., 8–15.

15. John W. Boudreau, *A Global Talent Marketplace: IBM's Global Workforce Initiative* (Washington, DC: Society for Human Resource Management, 2010).

16. Hoshein Arsham, *Decision Making in Economics and Finance*, http://home.ubalt.edu/ntsbarsh/Business-stat/stat-data/Forecast.htm#rappl Indexnu.

Chapter 5

1. John W. Boudreau, *A Global Talent Marketplace: IBM's Global Workforce Initiative* (Washington, DC: Society for Human Resource Management, 2010).

2. Tuomas Sandholm, David Levine, Michael Concordia, Paul Martyn, Rick Hughes, Jim Jacobs, and Dennis Bragg, "Changing the Game in Strategic

Sourcing at Procter & Gamble: Expressive Competition Enabled by Optimization," *Interfaces* 36, no. 1 (January–February 2006): 55–68.

3. Craig Schneider, "The New Human Capital Metrics," *CFO Magazine*, February 15, 2006, 1.

4. John Sullivan, "Best Recruiting Practices from the World's Most Business-Like Recruiting Function, Part 4," September 10, 2005, http://www .drjohnsullivan.com/content/view/89/27/.

5. Matthew Guthridge, Asmus B. Komm, and Emily Lawson, "The People Problem in Talent Management," *McKinsey Quarterly*, May 2006, 1.

6. Morgan W. McCall, Jr., and George P. Hollenbeck, "Global Fatalities," *Ivey Business Journal* 66, no. 5 (May/June 2002): 74–78.

7. Ram Reddy, "Taming the Bullwhip Effect," *Intelligent Enterprise*, June 13, 2001, http://intelligent-enterprise.informationweek.com/010613/ supplychain1_2.jhtml;jsessionid=EZN0PDZZA1SM5QE1GHPCKH4ATM Y32JVN.

8. Richard Metters, "Quantifying the Bullwhip Effect in Supply Chains," *Journal of Operations Management* 15, no. 2 (May 1997): 89.

9. "Doostang Seals Partnership with University of Virginia's Darden School of Business," Reuters online, April 8, 2009; http://www.reuters.com/ article/pressRelease/idUS123895+08-Apr-2009+MW20090408.

10. John W. Boudreau, *A Global Talent Marketplace*.

11. Ibid., 7.

Chapter 6

1. William Starbuck, "Unlearning Ineffective or Obsolete Technologies," *International Journal of Technology Management* 11, no. 7 (1996): 725–737, http://pages.stern.nyu.edu/~wstarbuc/unlearn.html.

2. Thanks to Peter Attfield of Unilever for the association with rapid prototyping.

3. Michael Schrage, *Serious Play* (Boston: Harvard Business School Press, 2000), 2.

4. Ibid., 19.

Index

Note: Page numbers preceded by *n* refer to notes.

accessibility, 100
accountability, 2, 179–194
    improved HR models and, 4
    in inventory optimization, 123
    market segmentation and,
        118–119
    in performance management,
        28–29
    of stakeholders, 183
    in supply-chain management,
        3–4
    talent life cycle and, 176–177
actionability, 100
adaptive questioning, 107
Aetna, 84–85
agility, 66–68
Air Canada, 95
alignment, 18–19
    time to build, 62–63
American Airlines, 14
Ameriprise Financial, 82–83,
        114–116, 124, 125, 127–128
analytics, 16–17

in aircraft production, 30–33
conjoint analysis, 101–104
constraint/bottleneck analysis,
        45–47
for developing economies, 73–83
Kano analysis, 35–40
on performance, 35–47
performance optimization and,
        25–55
risk–value analysis, 40–44
talent flow tools, 163–166
utility analysis, 52
Anand, Gopesh, *n*197
Anders, George, *n*198
Arsham, Hoshein, *n*199
Attfield, Peter, 53–54
AutoNation, 60–62, 68

backorder costs, 144
Bader, Rupert, 12
Baker, Stephen, 103, *n*195
Ballmer, Steve, 104, 123

Barringer, Melissa Woodard, *n*198

Bartlett, Christopher, *n*198

Baystate Health, 156–160

behavior, uncertainty of, 193–194

bell curve distributions, 48–49

bench strength tools, 166–168

Bock, Laszlo, 124

Boeing, 30–33

agility at, 68

constraint/bottleneck analysis
at, 45–47

Kano analysis of, 37–40

risk–value analysis of, 41–42

bottlenecks

in constraint analysis, 45–47

ROIP analysis and, 52–53

Boudreau, John, 16, 97, *n*195

Bragg, Dennis, *n*199

brand building, 75, 77–78, 81–83

brands, employment, 96–97

Brewer, M. B., 48–49

broadcast networks, 95

brokers, social network, 103

Bronson, John, 71–72

bullwhip effect, 169–171

business models

as common language, 19

transportation, 174–175

BusinessWeek, 12, 67

cafeteria benefits, 92–93

call centers, 58, 175

capacity, flexible, 174

Cappelli, Peter, 141, *n*199

career development, 139–140. *See
also* talent life cycle

career path tools, 166–168

Carey, Dennis, *n*196

Cascio, Wayne F., 97, *n*195, *n*196,
*n*198, *n*198

Cataphora, 102

central connectors, social
network, 103

Charnock, Elizabeth, 102

Chermak, Thomas J., *n*196

China, 73–74

collaboration, 77, 183–184, 187–189

Commonwealth Corporation,
158–159

communication, 3

about talent, 20

common language for, 19

improved HR models and, 4

models in facilitating, 11

competencies. *See also* performance
optimization

at Boeing, 32–33

competency systems on, 30

key/vital, 27

ROIP in retooling, 47, 50

in scenario planning, 65–66

time to build, 62–63

Concordia, Michael, *n*199

Conference Board CEO Challenge
Survey, 8–9

Conger, Jay A., *n*196

conjoint analysis, in talent supply
planning, 101–104, 118

designing alternatives in, 107

efficient frontier curve in,
111–113

matrix design in, 105–107

at Microsoft, 104–114

preference strength in, 108–109

response scales in, 107–108

reward costs/investments in,
109–111

constraint/bottleneck analysis,
    45–47
    in talent acquisition, 157–158
    on workforce flows, 164–166
Corning, 141
creativity
    innovation and, 191–193
    scenario planning and, 61
credibility, 188
Cross, Rob, 103
cultures
    collective, 100–101
    organizational, 14
Cummings, Melissa, 84–85
customer segmentation, in metrics
    analysis, 17, 102–103
customization, 92–96, 182

Darby, M. R., 48–49
Darden School of Business,
    170–171
data
    for business models, 19–20
    cost of poor/inaccurate, 171
    imperfect, 84–85, 86, 106
    improving use of, 16–17
    on recruitment and
        development, 152
    on turnover, 123–128,
        127–128
Davenport, Thomas O., n198
decision making, 180–181. See also
    accountability
    assumptions in, 14–15
    broader perspective in, 5–7, 12,
        151–154
    in HR versus other areas, 7–10
    improving HR, 4–7

information for, 10–11
    inventory optimization
        and, 135
    market segmentation and,
        117–119
    quality of, 183–184
dehumanization, 193–194
Delaney, K. J., n196
Dell, 174
demand, 144
    advanced logistics tools in,
        174–175
    bullwhip effect and, 169–171
    signals of, 169–174
demographics, employment deals
    and, 98–99
depletion
    as benefit, 136–139
    as benefit and cost, 139–140
    as cost, 133–135
derailers, talent development,
    167–168
developing economies
    strategic portfolio analysis for,
        73–83
    talent life cycle in, 152
differentiation, 186–187
Disneyland, 27
disruptions, minimizing, 5–6
diversification, workforce, 68–74
    China and, 73–74
    for multiple scenarios, 80–83
Doostang, 170–171

economic downturn, talent invest-
    ments and, 8–9
efficient frontier curve, 111–113
80-20 rule, 55, 187

employees. *See also* talent life cycle
  agile learners, 67–68
  benefit plans for, 92–96
  career development choices of,
    151–153
  engagement of, 114–116, 127–128
  generational differences among,
    98–99, 100–101, 137–139
  identifying vital, 2, 27, 46–47
  pivotal, 91
employment brands, 96–97
employment deals, 90–120
  at Ameriprise, 114–116
  conjoint analysis of, 101–114
  customized versus standardized,
    93–94
  demographics and preferences in,
    98–99
  designing, 90–91
  HR leaders and, 116–118
  mass-customization of, 92–96
  at Microsoft, 104–114
  ROI calculation on, 97–98
  usage patterns of, 96–97
  value in exploring, 119–120
employment life cycle. *See* talent
  life cycle
Enders, Rom, 32
engagement, employee, 114–116,
  127–128
engineering performance
  optimization, 21–22, 180–181
  accountability in, 29
  at Boeing, 30–33
  constraint/bottleneck analysis in,
    45–47
  Kano analysis in, 35–40
  reframing work performance as,
    33–35
  risk–value analysis in, 40–44
  targeting areas in, 33–35
Erickson, Tamara, 98, *n*198
Eustace, Alan, 50–51
Executive Office of Labor and
  Workforce Development,
  158–159
expertise taxonomy, 141, 171–174
experts, collaboration with, 188–189

Faber, Tracy, 51, *n*196
Fairhurst, David, 137
Farm Journal, 95
FedEx, 175
flexibility, 66–68
flow analysis tools, 163–166
forced-distribution performance
  systems, 27–28
free will, 10
Frito-Lay, 51–52

game theory, 83
Gates, Bill, 123
Gates, Stephen, *n*199
General Electric (GE), 1–2, 27–28
generational groups, 98, 101,
  137–139, 159
goal setting, in performance
  optimization, 28–29
Google, 50–51, 92, 124, 125
Guthridge, Matthew, *n*200

Hansen, Fay, *n*197
headhunters, 150
Hilbert, Dan, 160–161
Hill, T., *n*197

Hindman, Douglas Blanks, *n*198

hiring costs, 122, 125–127, 140, 142–145

holding costs, 144

Hollenbeck, George P., *n*200

HR. *See* human resources (HR)

HR Magazine, 137

hub-and-spoke systems, 175

Hughes, Rick, *n*199

human nature, 20–21
    assumptions about, 14–15
    free will and, 10

human resources (HR)
    allies for, 187–189
    collaboration with, 77, 187–189
    common ground with, 183–184
    enhancing strengths of, 7–11
    identity struggles in, 179–180
    importance of, 1–2
    improving decisions in, 4–7
    innovation and rapid prototyping
        in, 191–193
    job descriptions/inventories in,
        29–30
    metrics analysis in, 16–17
    need to retool, 11–17
    paradoxes in, 182
    portfolio diversification in,
        57–87
    retooled roles of, 180–194
    retooling with ROIP, 47–52
    risk-taking in, 184, 185
    ROI of programs in, 97–98
    segmentation and differentiation
        in, 186–187
    strategic partnerships with,
        15–16, 18–19
    strategic planning in, 189–191
    talent management tools, 96–99

unused data in, 114–116, 123–128

workforce logistics for, 175–176

IBM, 152, 164, 165
    Global Services, 140–142
    talent expertise taxonomy,
        171–174

iDeals, 94

identifiability, 99, 100

incentives, 1–2
    customized versus standardized,
        93
    influencing talent supply with,
        90–120
    mass customization of, 92–96
    at Microsoft, 104–114

inflection points, 184, 186
    in performance optimization,
        50–52
    scenario planning and, 61–62

innovation, 191–193

Institute for Healthcare
    Improvement, 156

inventory optimization, 12–13, 23,
    121–148
    broader perspective in, 151–154
    definition of, 122
    interlocking inventories in, 140,
        149–150
    on-demand workforce and,
        140–142
    principles in, 128–129
    questions in, 130–133
    reasons to hold inventory
        and, 143
    translating to workforce
        inventory, 144–145
    turnover statistics in, 123–128

inventory optimization (*continued*)
  when depletion is a benefit,
    136–139
  when depletion is a benefit and
    cost, 139–140
  when depletion is a cost, 133–135
investment decisions, 58, 180. *See
  also* portfolio theory
  for talent segmentation, 118
  workforce planning as, 81–83

Jackson, Michael, 60–62
Jacobs, Jim, *n*199
Jain, Mayank, 82, 83
job descriptions, 29–30. *See also*
  performance optimization
  at Boeing, 32–33
  identifying vital jobs and, 27,
    46–47, 91
  Kano analysis and, 39–40
  ROIP in retooling, 47, 50

Kallayil, Gopi, 92
Kamakura, Wagner Antonio,
  *n*198
Kano, Noriaki, 35, *n*196
Kano analysis, 35–40, 182
Karren, Ronald J., *n*198
key performance indicators (KPIs),
  30, 47, 50
Komm, Asmus B., *n*200
KPIs. *See* key performance
  indicators (KPIs)

Lane, Kevin, *n*197
Lawler, Edward, 16

Lawson, Emily, *n*200
leaders
  decision-making skill of, 183–184
  inventory optimization for,
    142–146
  market segmentation for,
    116–119
  portfolio optimization for, 83–86
  priority placed on talent by, 1–2
  ROIP use by, 47–54
  strategic HR partnerships with,
    15–16, 18–19
  talent life cycle and, 176–177
  time to build, 62–63
leadership allocation
  for China, 73–74
  for developing economies, 73–83
  pipelines for, 166–168
  portfolios in, 11–12
  ROIP analysis and, 53–54
  talent supply chains and,
    164, 166
leadership portfolios, 11–12
learning, agile, 67–68
legitimacy, 188
Levenson, Alec, 51, *n*196
Levine, David, *n*199
Levy, Martin, *n*197
Lincoln Electric, 100–101
Lindstadt, Hagen, *n*197
Linux, 48–49
logistics models, 12–13, 20, 152–153
  advanced tools in, 174–175
  demand signals in, 169–174
  guiding questions in, 155
  in metrics analysis, 17
  for succession planning, 168
  for talent life cycles, 149–178
Lunsford, J. L., 31

MacDonald, J. Randall, 172, *n*199

management. *See also* leaders

assumptions about human nature
in, 14–15

of people versus inventory, 20–21

of talent, 162–163

at Williams-Sonoma, 71–73

marketing

analytical frameworks in, 21

conjoint analysis in, 101–104

influencing talent supply and,
89–120

mass customization in, 94–96

market segmentation, 95–96

conjoint analysis for, 104–114

in talent planning, 99–101

Marriott, 95

Martyn, Paul, *n*199

McCall, Morgan, 167, *n*200

McDonald's, 42–44, 137–139

McFarland, Janet, *n*197

McKinsey & Company, 73

Meier, Penny, 114

mental models, 14–15, 17, 18

mentoring, 162–163

metrics, 5

constraint/bottleneck analysis,
45–47

improving, 16–17

Kano analysis, 35–40

mental models and, 17

risk–value analysis, 40–44

for ROIP, 35–47

in talent acquisition, 160–162

talent flow analysis tools,
163–166

talent life cycle, 189–190

on turnover, 13–14

usage patterns, 96–97

Metters, Richard, *n*200

Michaels, Daniel, *n*195

Microsoft, 12, 104–114, 123

Miller, S., *n*195

models. *See* business models;
mental models; talent models

Morrison, Scott, *n*199

motivation

employee benefits and, 92–96

mental models of, 14–15

open-source communities and,
48–49

Müller, Jürgen, *n*197

O'Connell, Jamie, *n*198

on-demand workforces, 140–142

Ontario Power Generation (OPG),
69–71, 73

open-source communities of
practice, 48–49

operations management,
143, 150

opportunities

missed, 58–59

turnover as, 125–127

optimization, 21

dehumanization and, 193–194

inventory, 12–13, 23

market, 95–96

performance, 25–55

of product design, 104

of risk, 40–44

supply chain, 3–4

of synergy, 23

of talent segmentation, 89–120

of workforce decisions, 141–142

in workforce planning, 22

ordering costs, 144

paradoxes, finding, 182
Parker, Ron, 67
Patsualos-Fox, Michael, *n*196
Pepsi, 67
performance, 6
  at Boeing, 32–33
  connecting to business
    outcomes, 54
  distributions of, 48–49
  engineering optimization,
    21–22
  forced-distribution systems in,
    27–28
  generational differences in,
    137–139
  key indicators of, 30, 180–181
  predicting, 10
  quality and quantity, 35
  return on improved, 26, 35–55
  70-20-10 systems for, 27–28,
    48–49
  targeting key, 33–35,
    48–52, 181
  tolerances in, 33–35
  turnover data and, 13–14,
    127–128
performance management
  systems, 30
performance optimization, 25–55
  in aircraft production, 30–33
  constraint/bottleneck analysis
    for, 45–47
  focus in, 26–29
  goal setting in, 28–29
  Kano analysis in, 35–40
  risk–value analysis in, 40–44
  utility analysis for, 52
peripheral players, social network,
  103

perspective
  in decision making, 5–7, 12
  in inventory optimization,
    151–154
  outsider, value of, 189
  on talent life cycle, 151–154,
    176–177
  on turnover, 126–128, 146–147
Pfeffer, Jeffrey, 14, *n*195
PFF Bank & Trust, 93
Pinder, Craig, *n*195
placement services, 150
play, 191–193
Pollner, Florian, *n*197
portfolio theory, 11–13, 57–87
  on China, 73–74
  for developing economies, 73–83
  finding and using risk in, 60–62
  focus in, 84
  in metrics analysis, 17
  scenario planning and, 59–60
  talent diversification in, 68–74
  talent risk in, 62–69
  uncertainty and agility in,
    66–68
  in workforce planning, 83–85
predictions. *See also* scenario
    planning
  based on the past, 63–64
  satisfaction points in, 78–80
  uncertainty in, 79–80
Procter & Gamble, 154
product design, 104
production rates, 144
prototyping, rapid, 191–193

quality improvement, 160
questioning, adaptive, 107

Ramstad, Peter, *n*195, *n*196

Ready, Douglas A., *n*196

recruitment, 150. *See also* talent
supply

bullwhip effect and, 170–171

costs of, 133, 136–139

projections in, 7

qualified applicants for, 152–153

Reddy, Ram, *n*200

Reingold, Jennifer, 103

research, investments in, 118

resource allocation, 163

response scales, 107–108

responsiveness, 100, 109

return on improved performance
(ROIP), 26

agility and, 67–68

at Boeing, 41–42

business leader use of, 52–54

constraint/bottleneck analysis
for, 45–47

definition of, 35

in developing economies, 75,
78–80

distribution curves in, 48–52

how to measure, 191

HR use of, 47–52

key performance indicators and,
47, 50

measuring, 35–47

open-source communities and,
48–49

risk–value analysis of, 40–44

utility analysis for, 52

at Williams-Sonoma, 72

return on investment (ROI), 35,
97–98

Reuters Online, 170–171

Riordan, Christine M., *n*197

risk management

at Boeing, 31–33

in developing economies, 73–80

finding and using risk in, 60–62

game theory and, 83

in human resources, 184, 185

inventory optimization and,
132–133

portfolio diversification in, 57–87

retooled approach to, 185

scenario-based, 59–60

workforce diversification and,
68–74

risk–value analysis, 40–44

Roberts, Darryl R., *n*198

ROIP. *See* return on improved
performance (ROIP)

Rousseau, Denise, 93–94, *n*197

Ryan, John R., *n*197

safety stock, 144

Sanders, Peter, *n*195, *n*196

Sandholm, Tuomas, *n*199

SAS Institute, 97

satisfaction points, 78–80

scenario planning, 59–60

on China, 73–74

for developing economies,
73–83

diversification for multiple
scenarios in, 80–83

finding and using risk in, 60–62

game theory and, 83

generic attributes in, 65–66

matrices in, 82, 85

multiple scenarios in, 80–83,
86–87

rethinking risk in, 185

scenario planning (*continued*)

  scenario selection in, 64–65, 83–84

  talent diversification in, 68–74

  on talent life cycle, 190

  talent risk in, 62–69

  uncertainty and agility in, 66–68

  at Williams-Sonoma, 71–73

  in workforce planning, 81–86

Schneider, Craig, *n*200

Schrage, Michael, 192, *n*200

segmentation, 186–187

  conjoint analysis for, 104–114

  customer, 17, 102–103

  human resources differentiation and, 186–187

  market, 95–96, 118–119

  talent, defining, 99–101

  talent, stakeholders and, 117–118, 120

  talent planning and, 99–101

Seraku, Nobuhiku, *n*196

Serious Play (Schrage), 192

70-20-10 system, 27–28, 48–49

Shah, Shamir, *n*198

shortage costs, 144

Slade, L. Allen, *n*198

social networks, 102–103

specification-driven approach, 192–193

stability, 100

staffing, as supply chain, 156–162

stakeholders

  accountability of, 2

  collaborative mind-set for, 183–184

  in developing economies, 76–77

  improving HR connections with, 54–55, 117–118

inventory optimization and, 148

portfolio optimization and, 87

talent life cycle and, 178

talent segmentation and, 117–118, 120

talent supply chains and, 164, 166

Starbuck, William, *n*200

Starbucks, 42–44, 82

stock-keeping units (SKUs), 173–174

strategic planning, 189–191

strategic uniqueness, 65–66

substantiality, 99, 100

succession planning, 162–163, 168

Sullivan, John, *n*200

supply-chain management

  advanced logistics tools in, 174–175

  at Boeing, 30–33

  bullwhip effect and, 169–171

  career development as, 162–163

  career paths as, 167–168

  conjoint analysis for, 101–104

  focus in, 27

  guiding questions in, 155

  in metrics analysis, 17

  staffing and, 156–162

  succession as, 162–163

  talent life cycle and, 150

  talent supply and, 89–120

  transparency and accountability in, 3–4

Swanson, Richard, *n*196

synergy optimization, 23

Takahashi, Fumio, *n*196

talent life cycle, 23, 149–178

talent life cycle (*continued*)
advanced logistics tools for, 174–175
at Baystate Health, 156–160
broader perspective on, 151–154, 176–177
career development and, 162–163
flow analysis tools for, 163–166
fluidity in, 63
guiding questions in optimizing, 155
interconnected inventories in, 149–150
inventory optimization and, 139–140
logistics optimization of, 152–154
rethinking risk in, 185
retooling tools on, 166–168
strategic planning for, 189–191
succession and, 162–163
supply chains in retooling, 156–162
talent sources in, 152–154
at Valero Energy, 160–162
workforce logistics for, 175–177
talent models
accessibility of, 11
decisions based on, 1–24
talent pipeline
combining multiple, 23–24
conjoint analysis planning for, 101–104
definition of, 11
talent supply
broader perspective on, 151–154
cost reduction goals and, 125–127
employment deals and, 90–120
hiring costs and, 122

interconnected inventories in, 149–150
inventory optimization and, 121–148
on-demand workforce and, 140–142
rethinking risk in, 185
shortages in, 123
talent life cycle and, 150
Tam, P. W., *n*196
television, customization in, 95
Towers Perrin, 105
Tsuji, Shinichi, *n*196
training programs, 136–139, 158–159
transparency, 3–4
transportation models, 174–175
turnover. *See also* inventory optimization
benchmark versus optimal levels of, 124–125
broader perspective on, 126–128, 146–147
data on, 123–128
definition of, 11, 123
for HR leaders, 142–145
internal, 139–140
metrics on, 13–14
at Microsoft, 109–111
as opportunity, 125–127
predicting, 10
questions about, 147
retooling analysis of, 130–142
Tyler, Richard, *n*199

uncertainty. *See also* risk management
agility and, 66–68

uncertainty (*continued*)
   of behavior, 193–194
   in developing economies, 73–83
   inventory optimization and,
     136–139
   in portfolio logic, 84–85
   in predictions, 79–80
Unilever, 53–54
University of Virginia, 170–171
usage patterns, 96–97
U.S. Bureau of Labor Statistics, 124
U.S. Conference Board, 123–124
Useem, Michael, *n*196
utility analysis, 52
utilization levels, 3

Valero Energy, 160–162, 175–176
Verizon, 126–127

Walker, Garrett, *n*199
Wall Street Journal, 124
Walmart, 13, 51, 125–126
Ward, Peter T., *n*197
Wedel, Michel, *n*198
Weigand, Kenneth, *n*198
Weinstein, Art, *n*198
Welch, Jack, 1–2, 27–28
Williams-Sonoma, 71–73

workforce creation, 131
workforce flow tables, 164–166
workforce planning, strategic, 22
   based on the past, 63–64
   for developing economies,
     73–83
   influencing supply in, 89–120
   on-demand workforce, 140–142
   portfolio diversification for,
     57–87
   ROIP analysis and, 53–54
   scenario-based, 59–62
   selecting probable future in,
     64–65
   social networks and, 102–103
   strategies in, 80
   supply-management in,
     156–162
   supply side, 22
   talent diversification in, 68–74
   talent risk in, 62–69
Wozny, Meg, *n*198

Yang, Lia Lynn, 103
YouTube.com, 95
Young, Mary, *n*196, *n*197, *n*199

Zucker, L. G., 48–49

About the Author

John W. Boudreau, PhD, Professor and Research Director at the University of Southern California's Marshall School of Business and Center for Effective Organizations, is recognized for breakthrough research on how decisions about human capital, talent, and human resources affect sustainable competitive advantage. He has more than fifty books, articles, and chapters published in *Management Science*, *Academy of Management Executive*, *Journal of Applied Psychology*, *Personnel Psychology*, *Asia-Pacific Human Resource Management*, *Human Resource Management*, *Journal of Vocational Behavior*, *Human Relations*, and *Industrial Relations*, with features in *Harvard Business Review*, the *Wall Street Journal*, *Fortune*, *Fast Company*, and *BusinessWeek*. His books include *Beyond HR*, with Peter Ramstad (Harvard Business School Publishing, 2007), *Investing in People*, with Wayne Cascio (Pearson, 2008), and *Achieving Excellence in Human Resource Management*, with Edward Lawler (Stanford University Press, 2009). Boudreau holds a BBA from New Mexico State University and a master's in management and PhD in industrial relations from Purdue University's Krannert School of Management. http://www.marshall.usc.edu/ceo/members/john-w-boudreau.htm.